Weight Watchers* Cookbook*

Editor: Pamela Dixon

Consultants: Barbara Hardwick & Beryl Hamilton
        WeightWatchers U. K.

Photography: John Dixon

Home Economist: Joy Machell

Tableware and kitchen accessories by Habitat and
Pamela Dixon

Acknowledgments:
The publishers wish to thank all of the members and staff of
WeightWatchers U.K. who contributed many of the creative
recipes, with a special thanks to Felice Lippert, Vice
President – Food Research, and her staff at WeightWatchers
International's headquarters for their guidance.

Published by
WeightWatchers Publications
635/637 Ajax Avenue,
Slough,
Berkshire

First published in 1978. Reprinted 1979 and 1980.

ISBN 450040267

Printed and bound in Great Britain by
Redwood Burn Limited, Trowbridge and Esher

WEIGHTS AND MEASURES

In the recipes, metric equivalents are given in brackets, rounded off to
the nearest 10 grammes (solids) and 10 millilitres (liquids). Liquids are
given in fluid ounces where this corresponds with measures used in the
Programme, but pints and tablespoons have been retained for simplicity
when measuring very large or very small amounts of water, etc. Eggs are
now sold in the EEC sizes, and we recommend that size 4 or 5 should be
bought to correspond to the 'standard' eggs referred to in the
Programme.

CONVERSION TABLE

Ounces/fluid ounces	Approx g. and ml. to nearest whole figure	Recommended conversion to nearest unit of 10
1	28	30
2	57	60
3	85	80
4	113	110
5 (¼ pint)	142	140
6	170	170
7	198	200
8 (½ lb.)	226	230
9	255	260
10 (½ pint)	283	280
11	311	310
12	340	340
13	368	370
14	396	400
15 (¾ pint)	428	430
16 (1 lb.)	456	460
17	484	480
18	512	510
19	541	540
20 (1 pint)	569	570

Contents

Introduction

Leave this book on the table, open at one of the colourful illustrations, next time you have visitors. Let your friends leaf through the pages, spotting ideas for delicious main courses, soups or desserts. They'll be astonished when they discover that these enticing recipes are all designed to fit into the Weight Watchers Programme.

Overweight people, it used to be believed, had to eke out a miserable existence if they wanted to become slim, giving up almost every food they'd ever enjoyed and keeping away from any social gathering in case temptation proved too much for them.

The Weight Watchers Organisation has changed all that. It has proved that if you eat the *right foods* in the *right quantities* you can follow an eating programme which is astonishingly varied and satisfying. It includes many of the items previously regarded as forbidden for fat people: you can eat the satisfying things like bread, potatoes and spaghetti, and even include flour in some of your dishes, providing you stick to the right amount and follow the correct 'patterns' for your meals.

This concept of eating well to get slim, instead of starving yourself, was new to this country when the Weight Watchers Organisation opened their first UK classes in 1967. But it worked. And not only did fat people become slim – they *stayed* slim. Their former attempts at losing weight had often been based on sporadic crash dieting – a system doomed to failure because, after losing weight, they would pick up their old habits of eating too much of the wrong foods and soon they would be right back where they started. Pills and injections gave similar short-lived benefits. But when overweight people joined Weight Watchers classes and began to enjoy living with a sensible eating programme, they realised that at last it was possible to achieve a weight loss which was permanent.

Many of the recipes in this book have been developed by British members of the Weight Watchers Organisation. Exchanging recipes and ideas with fellow class members has always been one of the ways in which they can help each other. Some people wonder why members attend classes, why they do not simply learn about eating the right foods and then take it from there! The answer lies in the mutual support which members give each other, plus of course the help and advice from trained lecturers at each weekly class. Most people find it hard to re-educate themselves and establish new eating habits. If they are tackling the problem on their own, they inevitably find it more difficult to follow a programme. This slows up their weight loss, they get discouraged and success hangs in the balance. Meeting fellow members *talking* about their temptations, and solving the problems together, they draw strength from the common objective of getting slim and staying that way! That in itself helps to stiffen their resolve.

Just why does the Weight Watchers Programme work so well? It works because it has been scientifically designed to provide you with choices needed to help you lose weight and keep your body in good working order. And by skilfully interpreting these requirements and using a wide range of ingredients, the Weight Watchers Organisation found that at last you can eat sensibly, lose weight *and* enjoy your food at the same time.

It's no coincidence that successful members of the Weight Watchers Organisation, besides looking slim, look healthy and happy as well. The Weight Watchers Programme is based on the most up-to-date medical and scientific research and is backed by nutritionists of international repute. With the Programme's insistence on three square meals a day, you need never be hungry. Indeed, you will sometimes find that you are eating *more* than you did before, from a greater variety of nutritious and satisfying foods that keep you fit while allowing a steady weight loss.

Once you have achieved your goal weight at Weight Watchers classes, you can learn to follow the Maintenance Plan, a carefully supervised 8 week course which shows you how to add to your daily eating plan. You will learn how to take the occasional drink, eat jam or have a piece of chocolate cake without putting weight on again because the Programme has become part of your life.

Entertaining has always been a problem for those concerned about their weight. It's impossible to cook and serve an exciting meal for other people and have to peck at it yourself! But with the help of the Weight Watchers Cookbook you will be able to serve delicious, colourful and nutritious dishes to family and friends without having to enter into any explanations. They simply won't be necessary because the food looks and tastes so good.

Together, the Weight Watchers Programme and your Weight Watchers class can teach you to lose excess weight and to keep it off for life. This book shows that while you're achieving your goal weight you can eat meals you'll really enjoy. You need not return to bad old habits, for this is the 'right food' you'll be happy to stay with for always.

Please read through carefully before you proceed. Remember to eat only the foods listed on your menu plan—in the quantities and weight specified.

CAUTION

Weight Watchers strongly advises you to consult your doctor while participating in the Programme and encourages a programme of periodical medical check-ups without indulging in self-medication. If you are under a doctor's care, you should have his written permission to follow the Programme. If you are or become pregnant, and are attending Weight Watchers classes, you must submit a doctor's written permission to participate in the Programme.

MORNING MEAL

Fruit, 1 serving
Choice of:
Egg, 1 or
Cheese, soft, 2½ oz.
or Cheese, semi-soft or hard, 1 oz
or
Cereal, 1 oz, with ½ milk serving or
Fish, cooked, 2 oz.
or
Poultry or Meat, cooked, 1 oz.
Bread, 1 serving
Beverage, if desired

MIDDAY MEAL

Choice of:
Poultry, Meat or Fish, cooked, 3-4 oz.
or Eggs, 2 or
Cheese, soft, 5 oz
or
Cheese, semi-soft or hard, 2 oz or
Dried Peas/Beans, cooked, 6 oz
Vegetables
Bread, 1 serving, if desired (2 for men and teenagers)
Beverage, if desired

EVENING MEAL

Choice of:
Poultry, Meat or Fish, cooked
Women and Teenagers 4–6 oz
Men 6–8 oz, or
Dried Peas/Beans, cooked
Women and Teenagers 8 oz
Men 12 oz

DAILY

Milk, 2 servings at any time
Fats, 3 servings, at mealtime
Fruits, 3 servings (3 to 5 for men and teenagers), 1 at Morning Meal, 2 at any time

The Midday Meal may be interchanged with the Evening Meal.

Fruits

FRUITS

Women
3 servings daily
Men
3-5 servings daily
Teenagers
3-5 servings daily

One serving *must* be taken at the Morning Meal. Select at least one daily from fruit marked with an asterisk (*). Vary selections.
Use fresh, canned or frozen fruit, or fruit juice, *with no sugar added.*

Eggs and Cheese

EGGS

Select 4 standard eggs a week (Size 4/5)

CHEESE

Soft Cheese
Examples: Cottage, Curd, skim milk Ricotta.
Semi-soft and Hard Cheese
Limit to 4 oz weekly
Examples of semi soft cheeses: Brie, Camembert, Danish Blue.
Examples of hard cheeses: Caerphilly, Cheddar, Cheshire, Edam, Gruyere, Leicester.

Dry and Liquid Measure Equivalents

Less than ⅛ teaspoon	Dash	
1½ teaspoons	½ tablespoon	¼ fl. oz
3 teaspoons	1 tablespoon	½ fl. oz.
2 tablespoons		1 fl. oz.
4 tablespoons		2 fl. oz.
8 tablespoons		4 fl. oz.
12 tablespoons	*NOTE: all measurements*	6 fl. oz.
16 tablespoons	*must be level*	8 fl. oz.

Milk

MILK

Women
2 servings daily
Men
2 servings daily

Teenagers
3-4 servings daily

Select servings at any time.
milk, skim
½ pint (10 fl oz)
buttermilk
½ pint (10 fl oz)
yogurt, natural, unsweetened
5 fl oz
The skim milk may be made from nonfat dry milk or may be commercially prepared liquid skim milk.

Bread, Cereal, Choice Group

Bread, Rolls and Baps
Women
2 servings daily
Men
4 servings daily
Teenagers
4 servings daily

Ordinary white or whole grain bread, rolls or baps 1 oz per serving. One serving *must* be taken at Morning Meal, unless Cereal or Choice is selected. If desired, once a week omit 2 servings and select one of the following: crumpet, English muffin, hamburger bap, scone, bagel or similar type bread.

Cereal

Select up to 3 times weekly, if desired. When cereal is taken, bread may be taken at Morning meal or another meal. Cereal must be eaten with at least ½ milk serving.
ready-to-eat (not pre-sweetened)
1 oz
uncooked
1 oz

Choice Group

Omit 1 serving of bread and select one item from this list up to 3 times weekly if desired.
barley
4 oz cooked
buckwheat groats (kasha)
1 oz dry
corn
ear, 1 medium
whole kernel or cream style
3 oz.
cornmeal
1 oz dry
cracked wheat (bulgur)
1 oz dry
hominy grits
6 oz cooked
pasta (macaroni, spaghetti or noodles)
3 oz cooked
potato, fresh or canned raw or cooked 3 oz
rice
white, brown or wild
3 oz cooked

Poultry, Meat, Fish, Dried Peas/Beans

Select daily from these groups. See Menu Plan for serving sizes. **NOTE:** if smoked poultry, meat or fish, or cured meat, is selected, *use the lower range* of the serving size.

Poultry, Veal, Game
Select chicken, turkey, other poultry (not duck or goose), veal or wild game. Serve poultry with skin removed.

'Beef' Group
Beef, Ham, Lamb, Pork, Tongue
Select up to 3 times weekly, if desired. Use lean meat. Remove visible fat before eating.

Select once a week, if desired, in place of one 'Beef' Group selection: bologna, frankfurters, knackwurst, beef sausages, or offal

Liver
Select once a week

Fish
Select any fish in the market place at least 3-5 times weekly. Vary selections. Use fresh, frozen, canned

or smoked fish. All canned fish must be well-drained. It is *strongly recommended* that 5 fish meals be eaten weekly. However, if fish is selected 3 or 4 times per week, chicken must be substituted for the one or two fish meals which have been omitted.

Dried Peas/Beans
Select up to 3 times weekly, if desired.
beans
butter, kidney, pink, soya beans or white (dried or canned dried)
lentils
(dried or canned dried)
peas
black-eyed (cowpeas)
chick (garbanzos) or split
(dried or canned dried)

Vegetables

Serving Size: 3 oz
Select at least 2 servings daily. Vegetables *must* be eaten at the Midday and Evening meals. They may also be eaten at any other time. Vary selections. Select a

reasonable number of servings of raw or cooked vegetables.
Limited Serving Size: 4 oz
The following vegetables are optional and must be weighed. Do not exceed a combined

total of 4 oz drained weight, daily.
artichoke (Jerusalem artichoke, globe artichoke, artichoke hearts)
beetroot,
broad beans
Brussels

sprouts
mange–tout
leeks
okra
onions
parsnips
peas
pumpkin
spring onion
swede

water chestnuts

NOTE: Do not include vegetables listed in Choice Group.

Fats   Optional

Select 3 servings daily at mealtime only.
Margarine, special (high in polyunsaturates)
1 level teaspoon
Margarine, low-fat spread (imitation)
2 level teaspoons
Mayonnaise
1 level teaspoon
Vegetable Oil
(corn, cottonseed, safflower, sesame, soyabean, sunflower)
1 level teaspoon.

Beverages
Water. Artificially sweetened carbonated beverages, soda water, coffee and tea in reasonable amounts.
Bonus
Select up to 1 serving daily, if desired.
mixed vegetable juice
8 fl oz
tomato juice
8 fl oz
tomato double concentrated purée or paste
2 oz

Seasonings and Condiments
Use reasonable amounts of the following: artificial

sweeteners, baking powder, baking soda, browning sauce, dehydrated vegetable flakes, essences, flavourings, herbs, horse-radish, hot sauce, lemon juice, lime juice, mustard, pepper, pepper sauce, rennet tablets, salt, seasonings, seaweed, soy sauce, spices, steak sauce, vinegar and Worcester sauce.

Something Extra
Select up to 3 servings daily, if desired.
arrowroot, cornflour, flour
1 level teaspoon
bouillon and stock
stock cube 1
stock powder

1 level teaspoon
cocoa, unsweetened
1 level teaspoon
concentrated yeast extract
1 level teaspoon
gelatine unflavoured
½ envelope (about 1½ level teaspoons)
ketchup, chilli sauce
2 level teaspoons
seeds:
caraway, poppy, sesame
1 level teaspoon

Speciality Foods
Members generally need not be concerned about counting calories (Kj). However if the following items are used calories (Kj)

MUST be counted. Limit intake to a total of 15 calories (65 Kj) per day. Check labels carefully for calorie count. *Do not use if label does not indicate calories (Kj)*
beverages, noncarbonated, low calorie (Kj)
salad dressings, low calorie (Kj)
jam, low calorie (Kj)
In addition, one serving of the following item may be substituted once daily, for one milk serving:
flavoured milk desserts low calorie (Kj)
4 oz

Fruit Servings

One serving *must* be taken at the Morning Meal. Select at least one daily from fruit marked with an asterisk (*). Vary selections. Use fresh, canned or frozen fruit, or fruit juice, with *no sugar* added.

Juices
*grapefruit 4 fl oz
*orange 4 fl oz
*orange and grapefruit 4 fl oz
prune 2½ fl oz
*tomato or mixed vegetable juice 8 fl oz

Fruits
apple, 1 medium
apple, canned, 4 oz
apricots, fresh, 2 medium
canned, 4 halves with 2 tablespoons juice
banana, ½ medium

Berries
blackberries, 5 oz
blueberries 5 oz
boysenberries 5 oz
cranberries 5 oz
gooseberries 5 oz

loganberries 5 oz
raspberries 5 oz
*strawberries 5 oz

*canteloupe, ½ medium or 5 oz chunks or balls
cherries, fresh, 10 large or 15 small, canned 4 oz
*currants, fresh, black, red or white 3 oz
damsons 4 small or 3 large
figs, fresh, 2 small
fruit cocktail or salad, 4 oz
*grapefruit ½ medium
*grapefruit sections 4 oz
grapes 12 medium or 20 small
*honey dew or similar melon 2″

wedge or 5 oz chunks or balls
*kiwi, (Chinese gooseberry) 1 medium
mandarin orange sections, canned 4 oz
mango ½ small
nectarine 1 medium
* orange 1 medium
*orange sections 4 oz
*papaya ½ medium
peach, fresh 1 medium
canned, 2 halves with 2 tablespoons juice, or 4 oz sliced
pear, fresh 1 small
canned, 2 halves with 2 tablespoons juice
persimmon 1 medium
pineapple, fresh,

¼ medium.
canned, chunks, crushed or tidbits 4 oz
canned, sliced 2 slices with 2 tablespoons juice
plums, fresh 2 medium
canned, whole 2 with 2 tablespoons juice
prunes, dried 4 medium or 3 large
rhubarb 9 oz
tangerine 1 large or 2 small
*ugli fruit 1 medium
watermelon 5 oz cubed or wedge 3″ × 1½″

Cooking Procedures

Eggs
May be cooked over direct heat, without fat, or in the shell.

Poultry and Game
May be boiled, poached, grilled, dry-fried, roasted or baked. Remove skin before eating.
If boiled with the skin, do not consume liquid. If boiled without skin liquid may be consumed. Refrigerate liquid, remove congealed fat. Six fluid ounces equals one serving of bouillon or stock.
If skin is removed, poultry or game may be browned in a non-stick pan or baked in a casserole with either raw or cooked ingredients. All ingredients may be consumed.

Veal
May be boiled,

grilled, dry fried, roasted or baked. If boiled, liquid may be consumed. Refrigerate liquid; remove congealed fat. Six fluid ounces equals one serving of bouillon or stock. If browned in a non-stick pan, a) transfer veal to another pan before adding raw or cooked ingredients or b) wipe pan clean before adding other ingredients.
If cooked in liquid (e.g. tomato juice or bouillon) veal must be removed from liquid with a slotted spatula. Whatever adheres to the veal may be consumed. Discard all other liquid. Only cooked veal may be used with added ingredients (e.g. casseroles, stews etc.) Liquid and added ingredients may be

consumed. Raw minced veal may be combined with other ingredients only if baked (not grilled) on a rack.

'Beef' Group
May be boiled or grilled, baked or roasted on a rack. If boiled, liquid may be consumed. Refrigerate liquid; remove congealed fat. Six fluid ounces equals one serving of bouillon or stock.
If grilled, baked or roasted on a rack, natural juices flowing from the meat during cutting may be consumed.
Raw minced meat may be consumed with other ingredients, only if baked (not grilled) on a rack. Cooked 'beef' may be used with added ingredients (e.g.

casseroles, stews, etc.) Liquid and added ingredients may be consumed.

Liver
May be boiled, poached, grilled, dry-fried or baked. Cooked or uncooked liver may be used with added ingredients (e.g. casseroles, stews, etc). Liquid and added ingredients may be consumed.

Fish
May be boiled, poached, grilled, dry fried, or baked. Cooked or uncooked fish may be used with added ingredients (e.g. casseroles, stews, etc.). Liquid and added ingredients may be consumed.

Dried Peas/Beans
Cook until tender.

Drain, reserving liquid if desired; weigh portions. Cooked dried peas/beans may be combined with other ingredients. Cooking liquid and added ingredients may be consumed.

Fats
May be mixed with other ingredients and baked in a casserole. May be melted over direct heat in flameproof container, or in a double boiler. After a food item has been grilled, pierce or cut lightly, if possible. Spread fat over food, and grill for no longer than one minute. May never be used for sautéing or frying.

Soups

Home-made soups are wonderful value – they are warming and nutritious and give creative cooks lots of scope for experiment. The lighter soups enable you to add an extra course to meals, while some of the more substantial ones make a main course on their own. And in the summer try delicious chilled soups with plenty of chopped fresh herbs – ideal for hot weather meals in the garden. Stock cubes are a good store cupboard standby, but try making your own stock as well, with the bones left from the chicken and plenty of flavouring herbs. (See p. 125) Finishing touch for your soups: a well chosen garnish to give a contrast in colour and texture. Choose from chopped parsley, sprigs of watercress, thin slices of lemon or finely chopped red or green peppers. Fingers of toast, or toasted croutons, from your bread allowance, go well with most soups. And treat yourself to a blender for soup making if you haven't got one already, but make sure that it's big enough – you'll find these recipes popular with the whole family.

Soups

Austrian Fish Soup

1 lb 2 oz (510 g) white fish fillet, skinned

3 pints (1 litre 700 ml) water

salt and pepper to taste

1 lemon

8 oz (230 g) onion, chopped

2 cloves garlic, crushed

3 × 1 oz slices bread (3 oz, 80 g) in cubes

3 oz (80 g) green pepper

3 oz (80 g) tomato

2 teaspoons Worcester Sauce, or to taste

6 oz (170 g) mixed prawns, mussels (cooked) and shrimps

2 tablespoons chopped parsley

Place fish in 4-pint saucepan, cover with water, add salt and pepper to taste and lemon cut in slices. Bring to boil and simmer until fish flakes easily with fork. Lift fish out and remove any bones. Flake fish, strain stock and return to pan. Add onion, garlic, bread, green pepper, tomato, Worcester sauce and fish and cook for 30 minutes. Add shellfish and cook for a further 5 minutes. Serve sprinkled with parsley. Divide into 3 equal portions.

Makes 3 servings

Broccoli Soup

6 oz (170 g) fresh or frozen broccoli

1 pint (570 ml) chicken stock made with 1 cube

1 oz (30 g) nonfat dry milk

salt and pepper to taste

Wash broccoli and cook in chicken stock until tender. Transfer to blender and blend until smooth. Add dry milk, blend for a further few seconds. Season and reheat before serving, but do not allow to boil. Divide into 2 equal portions.

Makes 2 servings

Cauliflower and Celery Soup

12 oz (340 g) celery, chopped and cooked

12 oz (340 g) cauliflower, cooked

10 fl oz (280 ml) chicken stock, made with 1 cube

2 teaspoons dried onion flakes

1 bay leaf

salt and pepper to taste

½ oz (15 g) nonfat dry milk

parsley for garnish

Put all vegetables in blender with stock and onion flakes and blend until smooth. Pour soup into saucepan and add bay leaf. Bring to boil and simmer gently for 5 minutes. Remove bay leaf, season to taste. Just before serving, whisk in the dry milk. Garnish with chopped parsley. Divide into 4 equal portions.

Makes 4 servings

Hungarian Thick Soup

1 × 15 oz (430 g) can celery hearts

3 oz (80 g) button mushrooms

1 pint (570 ml) chicken stock made with 1 cube

2 teaspoons paprika

¼ teaspoon dried tarragon

salt and pepper to taste

Place celery hearts and can liquid in blender and blend at high speed until smooth. Alternatively, mash very well with a fork. Slice the mushrooms, combine with stock, paprika, tarragon, salt and pepper and simmer until mushrooms are tender. Add blended celery hearts, bring to the boil and simmer for 2-3 minutes. Taste and adjust seasonings. Divide into 4 equal portions and serve hot.

Makes 4 servings

Carrot and Tomato Soup

12 oz (340 g) canned carrots

16 fl oz (460 ml) tomato juice

15 fl oz (430 ml) water

½ teaspoon garlic salt

1 teaspoon dried basil

1 chicken stock cube

ground black pepper to taste

4 teaspoons cornflour

2 teaspoons chopped parsley

Chop carrots and mix with tomato juice, water, garlic salt, basil, stock cube and pepper. Place half mixture in blender and run at high speed until reduced to a purée. Pour into saucepan. Repeat process with other half. Bring to the boil and simmer for 2 minutes. Mix cornflour with 2 tablespoons water, stir into soup and continue to cook for a further 3 minutes. Serve sprinkled with parsley. Divide into 4 equal portions.

Makes 4 servings

Cold Artichoke Soup

12 oz (340 g) canned artichoke hearts, drained weight

15 fl oz (430 ml) chicken stock made with 1 cube

¼ teaspoon dried oregano

2 tablespoons lemon juice

10 fl oz (280 ml) skim milk

salt and pepper to taste

paprika

Rinse artichokes thoroughly, place in blender with chicken stock and oregano, and blend. Add lemon juice, milk and seasoning. Chill. Sprinkle with paprika, divide into 4 equal portions and serve.

Makes 4 servings

Dumplings in Tomato Soup

Soup:

8 fl oz (230 ml) tomato juice

dash Worcester sauce

2 teaspoons nonfat dry milk

2 tablespoons cold water

salt and pepper to taste

Place all ingredients in a saucepan, cover with lid and cook slowly over low heat.

Dumplings:

3 teaspoons self-raising flour

1 slice bread (1 oz, 30 g) in crumbs

1 oz (30 g) Cheddar cheese, grated

salt and pepper to taste

1 teaspoon dried herbs (optional)

1 standard egg, beaten

Mix together flour, crumbs and $\frac{3}{4}$ oz (25 g) cheese. Add salt, pepper and herbs. Mix well and bind with egg. Shape into 4 small dumplings and add to the soup. Replace lid and simmer for 10 minutes. Sprinkle with remaining cheese before serving.

Makes 1 serving

Chilled Tomato-Orange Soup

10 fl oz (280 ml) natural unsweetened yogurt

10 fl oz (280 ml) tomato juice

4 fl oz (110 ml) orange juice

1-2 mint leaves

salt and pepper to taste

1 teaspoon lemon juice

chopped parsley for garnish

Place yogurt and tomato juice in blender. Blend well, then add orange juice, mint leaves, salt, pepper and lemon juice. Blend again and chill. Serve sprinkled with chopped parsley. Divide into 4 equal portions.

Makes 4 servings

Hearty Vegetable Soup

1 beef stock cube

6 oz (170 g) carrots, chopped

2 oz (60 g) onion, chopped

2 oz (60 g) cooked beetroot

4 large lettuce leaves

1 slice bread (1 oz, 30 g), toasted

2 oz (60 g) grated hard cheese

Make 1 pint (570 ml) stock with the cube, and cook carrots and onion in it until tender. Place in blender with beetroot and lettuce leaves and blend well. Return to saucepan and reheat. Sprinkle grated cheese on the toast and place under grill until cheese is melted. Cut toast into cubes and place in soup bowl. Pour soup over the toast and serve immediately.

Makes 1 serving

Cream of Vegetable Soup

2 chicken stock cubes

$1\frac{1}{4}$ pints (710 ml) water

2 teaspoons dried onion flakes

12 oz (340 g) celery, chopped

3 oz (80 g) green pepper, diced

8 fl oz (230 ml) skim milk

pepper to taste

Mix stock cubes, water, onion flakes and celery in a saucepan. Simmer for 20 minutes, remove from heat, transfer to blender and blend until smooth. Rub through a sieve, return to saucepan, add green pepper and simmer for 4-5 minutes. Add milk and pepper, reheat but *do not boil*. Divide into 4 equal portions.

Makes 4 servings

Winter Pea Soup

2 oz (60 g) onion, chopped

2 oz (60 g) celery, diced

2 oz (60 g) carrots, chopped

15 fl oz (430 ml) chicken stock made with 1 cube

4 oz (110 g) cooked split peas

2 oz (60 g) cooked ham, diced

pepper to taste

Place onion, celery and carrot in saucepan with stock and simmer until tender, but still crisp. Add peas, ham and pepper to taste and cook for a further 5 minutes until thoroughly heated. Serve piping hot.

Makes 1 serving

Special Italian Soup

1 pint (570 ml) beef stock made with 1 cube

4 oz (110 g) onion, chopped

3 oz (80 g) carrots, sliced

3 oz (80 g) courgettes, sliced

1 sachet dried bouquet garni (mixed thyme, parsley and bayleaf)

salt and pepper to taste

garlic powder to taste

3 teaspoons cornflour

6 oz (170 g) cooked pasta shells

chopped parsley for garnish

Place stock, onion, carrots, courgettes and *bouquet garni* in 2½ pint saucepan. Season with salt, pepper and garlic powder. Bring to boil and simmer for 15-20 minutes. Mix cornflour with 2 tablespoons water, add to soup and bring to the boil stirring constantly. Add pasta shells and allow to simmer for a further 5 minutes. Serve piping hot sprinkled with parsley. Divide into 2 equal portions.

Makes 2 servings

Watercress Soup

1 bunch watercress

10 fl oz (280 ml) chicken stock made with 1 cube

½ oz (15 g) non fat dry milk

freshly ground black pepper to taste

Wash the watercress, cut off discoloured ends of the stems and chop the remainder. Place the watercress in a saucepan with the stock. Bring to the boil and simmer for 10 minutes. Transfer to blender and run at high speed until smooth. Pour back into saucepan, stir in the dry milk, add pepper and reheat without boiling. Serve either piping hot or chilled, garnished with sprigs of watercress.

Makes 1 serving

Spanish Summer Soup

6 oz (170 g) tomatoes

6 oz (170 g) green pepper

6 oz (170 g) red pepper

2 cloves garlic

2 oz (60 g) onion

2 teaspoons vegetable oil

salt and pepper to taste

2 teaspoons cider vinegar

Skin and chop tomatoes, de-seed and chop peppers, crush garlic and chop onion. Reserve 2 tablespoons pepper and onion. Place rest of vegetables in the blender with a little water and purée until smooth. Pour into 2 serving bowls, divide oil and vinegar between bowls, add salt and pepper and stir. Chill well and garnish with the reserved vegetables. Serve at mealtime only.

Makes 2 servings

Cauliflower and Tomato Soup

18 oz (510 g) cauliflower

10 fl oz (280 ml) tomato juice

15 fl oz (430 ml) chicken stock made with 1 cube

salt and pepper to taste

3 oz (80 g) button mushrooms

1 teaspoon dried basil

1 tablespoon chopped parsley

Wash the cauliflower, including the outside green leaves, and cut into small pieces. Place in a saucepan with the tomato juice, stock, salt and pepper. Bring to the boil, cover pan and simmer for about 15 minutes or until the cauliflower is tender. Divide evenly between 4 soup bowls.

Makes 4 servings

Minty Green Pea Soup

8 oz (230 g) peas, fresh or frozen

1½ pints (scant litre) water

2 chicken stock cubes

2–3 sprigs mint

salt and pepper to taste

Combine the peas, water, stock cubes, mint and salt and pepper in a saucepan. Bring to the boil and simmer until peas are soft. Leave to cool, then purée in blender. Reheat when required, and divide evenly between 2 soup bowls.

Makes 2 servings

Hints and Tips

Parsley stalks have more flavour than the leaves. Use stalks in stock making and with the soup vegetables. Save the leaves to chop for garnish.

● Watercress and parsley are particularly useful in the winter months. To store for several days, buy them as fresh and green as you can. Wrap in plenty of paper towelling, then pop them into a plastic bag and place in the fridge, well away from the ice compartment.

● When serving dried peas or beans as a vegetable, cook an extra portion and refrigerate for soup the next day.

Left: Special Italian Soup

Vegetables and Salads

Your friends might believe that you are simply indulging yourself when they see the wonderful variety of vegetables and salads you can enjoy on the Weight Watchers Programme. As well as cooked vegetables, you will find raw, crunchy things like celery, cucumber or carrots invaluable for nibbling – they taste good and help to educate your palate away from stodgy, fattening snacks. And salads have come a long way from that tired lettuce plus tomato and cucumber routine. Members of the Weight Watchers Organisation have been quick to realise that almost any crisp vegetable or fruit can go into a salad, as you will see from these favourite recipes. There is also a growing interest today in non-meat dishes which may be used for main courses, either made entirely from vegetables or from vegetables combined with cheese or eggs. Protein-rich dried peas and beans may also be used for complete dishes. They are satisfying and tasty when cooked with skilfully chosen herbs and spices.

Vegetables and Salads

Artichokes in Tomato Jelly

1 tablespoon unflavoured gelatine

14 fl oz (400 ml) tomato juice

1 tablespoon Worcester sauce

½ teaspoon onion salt

½ teaspoon grated horseradish

salt and pepper to taste

16 oz (460 g) canned artichoke hearts, drained weight, quartered

4 slices lemon

parsley sprigs

Combine gelatine with 2 tablespoons tomato juice and stir over low heat until gelatine is dissolved. Stir in remaining tomato juice, Worcester sauce, onion salt, horseradish and salt and pepper. Chill until just beginning to set. Fold in artichoke hearts and divide jelly between 4 wine glasses. Chill until firm, decorate each with a twist of lemon and sprig of parsley.

Makes 4 servings

Baked Leek Special

4 oz (110 g) leeks

1 teaspoon margarine

2 teaspoons flour

¼ teaspoon nutmeg

1½ oz (45 g) boiled ham

3 oz (80 g) potato, baked or boiled in skin, sliced

1 oz (30 g) Swiss cheese, grated

Preheat oven to 350°F, Gas Mark 4, 180°C. Wash leeks thoroughly, cut into 4-5″ lengths. Boil in salted water for about 5 minutes, or until tender. Drain and reserve liquid. Melt margarine in top half of double boiler over boiling water. Stir in flour. Add 6 fl oz (170 ml) cooking liquid from the leeks and cook until thickened, stirring occasionally. Add nutmeg. Wrap thinly cut boiled ham round leeks and place in ovenproof dish. Cover with potatoes, then with sauce and sprinkle with grated cheese. Bake in oven for 15-20 minutes.

Makes 1 serving

Green Bean Salad

12 oz (340 g) fresh or frozen runner beans

6 oz (170 g) celery, diced

½ teaspoon dried onion flakes

6 oz (170 g) green pepper, de-seeded and chopped

6 oz (170 g) pickled cucumbers, chopped

6 oz (170 g) fresh cucumber, sliced

3 tablespoons tarragon vinegar

3 tablespoons white wine vinegar

artificial sweetener to taste

freshly ground black pepper to taste

Mix all ingredients in a large bowl, season well. Cover and chill overnight in refrigerator. Divide into 4 equal portions before serving.

Makes 4 servings

Barbecued Butter Beans

8 oz (230 g) cooked, dried butter beans, drained weight

2 oz (60 g) onion, sliced

4 tablespoons (2 oz, 60 g) tomato purée

4 fl oz (110 ml) chicken stock made with ½ cube

1 teaspoon Worcester sauce

⅛ teaspoon chilli powder or to taste

dash hot sauce

artificial sweetener to taste

Preheat oven to 350°F, Gas Mark 4, 180°C. Layer beans and onions in a casserole. Combine remaining ingredients, mix well and pour over bean mixture. Bake in oven for 30-40 minutes. Serve at once.

Makes 1 serving

French Beans Au Gratin

12 oz (340 g) tomatoes

4 oz (110 g) onion

artificial sweetener to taste

sprigs of parsley and thyme

1 bay leaf

salt and pepper to taste

12 oz (340 g) french beans, sliced

4 oz (110 g) hard cheese, grated

Dip tomatoes in boiling water, drain and skin. Roughly chop tomatoes and place in saucepan with thinly sliced onion, sweetener, herbs and seasoning. Cook gently until tender. Rub mixture through sieve. Reheat gently. Cook beans in boiling, salted water for about 6-8 minutes or until tender but still crisp. Drain and mix with tomato sauce. Place in a heatproof serving dish and cover with grated cheese. If desired, place under grill for 1 minute before serving. Divide into 2 equal portions.

Makes 2 servings

Cocktail Mushrooms

8 oz (230 g) button mushrooms

½ teaspoon salt

10 fl oz (280 ml) cider vinegar

6 peppercorns

¼ teaspoon dried onion flakes

1 sprig parsley

1 bay leaf

½ teaspoon celery salt

Wash mushrooms, discard stems and set mushroom caps aside. Meanwhile, combine all other ingredients and boil for 10 minutes. Pour over drained mushroom caps and cool. When cold, transfer to a jar, cover tightly and shake well. Refrigerate for at least 24 hours before using. Drain off liquid and divide mushrooms into 2 equal portions before serving.

Makes 2 servings

Duchess Potatoes

1 lb 2 oz (510 g) cooked, peeled potatoes

5 fl oz (140 ml) skim milk

6 teaspoons margarine

salt and pepper to taste

Preheat oven to 375°F, Gas Mark 5, 190°C. Mash potatoes thoroughly, beat in milk, margarine and seasoning. Put mixture into piping bag and pipe small rounds onto baking tray. Place in oven for 10-15 minutes until nicely browned. Divide into 6 equal portions and serve with roast meat.

Makes 6 servings

Cucumber Salad

½ lettuce

6 oz (170 g) cucumber

5 fl oz (140 ml) natural unsweetened yogurt

2 tablespoons mayonnaise

1 tablespoon lemon juice

salt and black pepper to taste

3 oz (80 g) red pepper

Wash and dry lettuce. Shred into small pieces and place in a bowl. Peel and dice cucumber, add to lettuce and mix well. Combine yogurt, mayonnaise and lemon juice. Season with salt and black pepper. Pour over lettuce and cucumber and toss well. Garnish with strips of red pepper. Divide into 4 equal portions and serve with meat or fish dishes. Serve at mealtime only.

Makes 4 servings

Golden Potato Salad

3 oz (80 g) cooked, peeled new potatoes

3 oz (80 g) canned sweetcorn, drained weight

2 oz (60 g) spring onions, chopped

2 teaspoons mayonnaise

dash Worcester sauce

Place potatoes, corn and spring onions in a bowl. Mix mayonnaise with Worcester sauce, pour over vegetables and toss together. Chill and divide into 2 equal portions before serving. Serve at mealtime only.

Makes 2 servings

Above left: Golden Potato Salad
Left: Coleslaw
Right: Cucumber Salad

Vegetables and Salads

Coleslaw

½ green or white cabbage, shredded

4 oz (110 g) onion, minced

3 oz (80 g) celery, chopped

3 oz (80 g) green pepper, chopped

3 oz (80 g) carrot, grated

2 oz (60 g) radishes, sliced

5 fl oz (140 ml) natural unsweetened yogurt

artificial sweetener to taste

2 teaspoons salt

2 tablespoons vinegar

4 oz (110 g) pineapple cubes, no sugar added

Mix the cabbage with 2 oz (60 g) onion and the celery, pepper, carrots and radishes. Mix yogurt, remaining onion, sweetener, salt and vinegar. Cover and refrigerate both mixtures. Combine just before serving and fold in pineapple cubes. Divide into 2 equal portions.

Makes 2 servings

Rice Lautrec

1½ oz (45 g) carrots, diced

1½ oz (45 g) peas

1½ oz (45 g) turnips, diced

1½ oz (45 g) swede, diced

1 oz (30 g) onion, diced

12 fl oz (340 ml) mixed vegetable juice

1 teaspoon dried mixed herbs

1 stock cube

2 oz (60 g) hard cheese, grated

3 oz (80 g) hot, cooked brown rice

Put carrots, peas, turnips, swede and onion in a 2-pint saucepan, add mixed vegetable juice, herbs and stock cube. Bring to boil, reduce heat, cover pan and simmer gently until vegetables are tender but still crisp. Meanwhile, prepare rice. Pour vegetable mixture over rice, sprinkle with grated cheese and serve at once.

Makes 1 serving

Savoury Cucumber

1 lb (460 g) cucumber

3 oz (80 g) celery, chopped

6 oz (170 g) cooked rice*

2 standard eggs

salt and black pepper to taste

dash hot sauce

4 oz (110 g) canned tuna, drained and flaked

1 tablespoon chopped parsley for garnish

Wash but do not peel cucumber. Cut through centre and then cut each half lengthwise. Scrape out seeds with a teaspoon. Cook cucumber and celery in boiling, lightly salted water for 10 minutes. Remove cucumber and set aside; continue cooking celery until tender. Drain celery and combine with rice. Lightly beat eggs, season and make into omelette. (See Omelette with Mushrooms and Peppers, p. 147, for method). Roll omelette up, cut into strips about ½″ wide and add to rice mixture. Add flaked tuna and mix well. Arrange cucumber boats on a serving dish and fill with rice mixture. Sprinkle with chopped parsley and serve well chilled. Divide into 2 equal portions.

*Prepare rice as follows:

10 fl oz (280 ml) water

3½ oz (95 g) uncooked rice

½ teaspoon salt

1 tablespoon dried onion flakes

Bring water to the boil in a saucepan. Add uncooked rice, salt and onion flakes. Cover tightly and simmer until all liquid is absorbed. Remove from heat. Weigh 6 oz (170g) cooked rice.

Makes 2 servings

Marrow Hot Pot

12 oz (340 g) marrow, peeled and sliced

6 oz (170 g) tomatoes, skinned and sliced

8 oz (230 g) onion, peeled and sliced

3 tablespoons chicken stock, made with ¼ cube

12 oz (340 g) potatoes, peeled weight

8 oz (230 g) Cheddar cheese, grated

salt and freshly ground black pepper

Preheat oven to 350°F, Gas Mark 4, 180°C. Cook marrow, tomatoes and onions in a non-stick pan with the stock for 5-10 minutes, stirring constantly. Par-boil potatoes in boiling, salted water for 10 minutes. Drain, cut into ¼″ slices. Arrange layers of vegetables in an ovenproof dish. Sprinkle cheese and seasoning between each layer. Finish with layer of potatoes and cheese. Bake in oven for 45 minutes. Brown under grill and divide into 4 equal portions before serving.

Makes 4 servings

Russian Tomato Salad

2 × 3 oz (80 g) tomatoes

1 tablespoon mayonnaise

2½ fl oz (70 ml) natural unsweetened yogurt

2 teaspoons chopped parsley

parsley sprigs for garnish

Skin the tomatoes and cut in half. Mix together mayonnaise and yogurt and add chopped parsley. Spoon yogurt mixture over tomatoes and chill well. Garnish with sprigs of parsley before serving. Serve at mealtime only.

Makes 1 serving

Sauerkraut

1 lb (460 g) white cabbage, shredded

4 oz (110 g) onion, chopped

1 clove garlic, crushed

4 tablespoons chicken stock made with ½ cube

1 tablespoon wine vinegar

2 teaspoons lemon juice

½ teaspoon caraway seeds

1 bay leaf

salt and pepper to taste

2 tablespoons margarine

Place cabbage, onion, garlic, stock, vinegar, lemon juice, caraway seeds, bay leaf and seasoning in saucepan. Bring to boil and simmer gently for about 10 minutes or until soft but still crisp. Meanwhile melt margarine in basin over hot water. When cabbage is cooked pour melted margarine over cabbage and transfer to hot serving dish. Divide into 4 equal portions.
Serve at mealtime only.

Makes 4 servings

Sardine and Beetroot Salad

8 oz (230 g) sardines, drained

6 oz (170 g) cooked beetroot

2 medium eating apples

4 teaspoons mayonnaise

lettuce

lemon juice

Mash drained sardines in a bowl, grate the beetroot and one apple and mix with sardines and mayonnaise. Beat all together. Serve on a bed of lettuce and garnish with remaining apple, sliced and sprinkled with lemon juice to prevent discoloration. Divide into 2 equal portions before serving.

Makes 2 servings

Vegetable Curry

1½ teaspoons coriander

1 teaspoon turmeric

½ teaspoon cumin

½ teaspoon ginger

½ teaspoon chilli powder

2 tablespoons onion flakes

1 medium cauliflower

1 lb (460 g) tomatoes, skinned

1 lb (460 g) carrots, diced

1 lb (460 g) broad beans, fresh or frozen

12 oz (340 g) potato, diced

2 tablespoons lemon juice

salt and pepper to taste

3-4 sprigs parsley

Make a paste with coriander, turmeric, cumin, ginger and chilli powder and 1 tablespoon cold water. Gradually add enough boiling water to give a large cupful, stirring all the time. Soak onion flakes, drain and dry-fry in non-stick pan until brown. Cut cauliflower into flowerets and set aside. Add curry spices and tomatoes to onions in pan, bring to boil. Add carrots, broad beans, potatoes, cauliflower, lemon juice, salt and pepper with just enough water to cover the vegetables. Stir well and bring to boil. Cover pan, simmer until vegetables are tender but still crisp, shaking occasionally to prevent sticking. Garnish with chopped parsley. Divide into 4 equal portions and serve as a starter or as an accompaniment to meat or poultry.

Makes 4 servings

Stuffed Cucumber

2 × 1 lb (460 g) cucumbers

12 oz (340 g) canned mushrooms, drained weight

2 oz (60 g) onion, finely chopped

salt and pepper to taste

nutmeg to taste

6 oz (170 g) tomatoes

Peel cucumbers, cut in half lengthwise and scoop out seeds. Place in a saucepan, cover with water and boil for about 4 minutes or until tender. Drain and set aside. Roughly chop mushrooms and finely chop onions. Place in basin, sprinkle with salt, pepper and nutmeg. Mix thoroughly. Divide evenly between cucumber boats. Halve tomatoes and scoop out seeds with a spoon, cut into thin strips and use as a garnish. Chill and divide into 4 equal portions before serving.

Makes 4 servings

Nibbler's Summer Lunch

8 fl oz (230 ml) tomato juice

2 teaspoons Worcester sauce

chopped parsley

2 sticks celery

1 oz (30 g) cooked beetroot

3 oz (80 g) carrots

2 oz (60 g) cucumber

1 oz (30 g) spring onions

2 oz (60 g) Edam cheese

3 oz (80 g) tomatoes

1 slice bread (1 oz, 30 g) toasted and spread with 1 teaspoon margarine

Mix tomato juice and Worcester sauce together and pour into a large glass. Sprinkle with chopped parsley and place in refrigerator to chill. Clean celery and cut into 3″ long pieces. Dice beetroot and use to fill the centre hollow of the celery. Cut carrots, cucumber, spring onions and Edam cheese into thin 3″ fingers. Quarter tomatoes. Arrange vegetables and toast on a large plate, alternating for colour. Serve with tomato juice.

Makes 1 serving

Left: Stuffed Cucumber
Above: Nibblers Summer Lunch

Vegetables and Salads

Chick Peas Neapolitan

6 oz (170 g) cooked, dried chick peas, drained weight

2 fl oz (60 ml) chicken stock made with ½ cube

¼ teaspoon oregano

pinch garlic powder

1½ oz (45 g) diced green or red pepper

pepper to taste

2 teaspoons margarine

Combine all ingredients, except margarine, in a saucepan and heat thoroughly. Just before serving, remove from heat, add margarine and toss lightly.

Makes 1 serving

Tomato and Lentil Supper

6 oz (170 g) tomatoes, skinned and chopped

3 oz (80 g) mushrooms, sliced

1 teaspoon dried onion flakes

1 lb (460 g) cooked split peas and lentils, mixed

salt and pepper to taste

2 teaspoons margarine

chopped chives

paprika

Dry-fry the tomatoes, mushrooms and onion flakes slowly in a saucepan. When soft add the split peas and lentils and heat thoroughly, stirring gently all the time. Season with salt and pepper. Turn into fireproof dish, dot with margarine and brown under grill. Garnish with chopped chives and sprinkle with paprika. Divide into 2 equal portions and serve with green salad.

Makes 2 servings

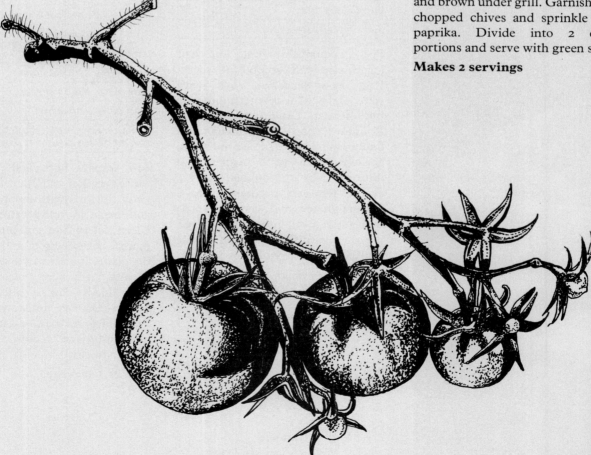

Vegetables and Salads

Tomatoes with Herb Cheese Stuffing

½ clove garlic

½ teaspoon dried dill weed

½ teaspoon chopped parsley

5 oz (140 g) curd cheese

4 × 2 oz (60 g) tomatoes

2 oz (60 g) Cheddar cheese

watercress for garnish

Crush the garlic. Mix garlic and herbs into the curd cheese, beating well with a fork. Cut tomatoes in half and scoop out centres. Divide cheese mixture evenly between the tomato 'cups'. Sprinkle with grated Cheddar cheese and garnish with watercress. Divide into 2 equal portions.

Makes 2 servings

Potato Salad

2 tablespoons dried onion flakes

12 oz (340 g) cooked, peeled potatoes

12 oz (340 g) cooked cauliflower

⅛ teaspoon celery seed

¼ teaspoon dry mustard

⅛ teaspoon coarsely ground black pepper

2 tablespoons wine vinegar

4 tablespoons mayonnaise

Cover onion flakes with boiling water and leave to soften. In bowl combine potatoes, cauliflower, celery seed, dry mustard, drained onion flakes and ground black pepper. Add vinegar gradually to mayonnaise, pour over the potato mixture and stir well. Divide into 4 equal portions.

Serve at mealtime only.

Makes 4 servings

Vegetable Cheese Polonaise

3 oz (80 g) cooked cauliflower

4 fl oz (110 ml) chicken stock made with ½ cube

2 teaspoons dried onion flakes

salt and pepper to taste

6 oz (170 g) cooked broccoli, chopped

1 slice white bread (1 oz, 30 g) made into crumbs

1 oz (30 g) hard cheese, grated

1 standard egg, hard-boiled and finely chopped

Preheat oven to 375°F, Gas Mark 5, 190°C. Place cauliflower, stock and onion flakes in blender. Blend until smooth, season to taste and mix with broccoli. Turn into a non-stick baking tin. Mix breadcrumbs with cheese and spread over vegetables. Bake in oven for 20 minutes or until vegetables are thoroughly hot and cheese has melted. Remove, sprinkle with chopped egg and serve at once.

Makes 1 serving

Salad Tomatoes

4 × 3 oz (80 g) tomatoes

4 oz (110 g) onion, finely minced

1 tablespoon parsley, chopped

2 tablespoons vegetable oil

2 tablespoons cider vinegar

¼ teaspoon pepper

¼ teaspoon salt

1 teaspoon dry mustard

artificial sweetener to taste

Halve tomatoes and arrange on serving dish. Mix onion and parsley and place an equal portion on top of each tomato half. Combine remaining ingredients and spoon over tomato halves. Divide into 4 equal portions. Serve at mealtime only.

Makes 4 servings

Tossed Green Salad

½ head cos lettuce

½ head round lettuce

1 bunch radishes, sliced

Green Dressing*

Wash lettuce and dry well. Break into bite-sized pieces. Add radish slices. Toss with Green Dressing and divide into 4 equal portions.

Makes 4 servings

*See p. 37 for dressing recipe

Cheese and Vegetable Bake

6 oz (170 g) potatoes, peeled weight

6 oz (170 g) onion

1 teaspoon vegetable or beef extract

1 teaspoon dry mustard

2 oz (60 g) hard cheese

5 oz (140 g) cottage cheese

salt and pepper to taste

pinch of mixed dried herbs

6 oz (170 g) tomatoes, sliced

mustard and cress for garnish

Preheat oven to 425°F, Gas Mark 7, 220°C. Cook potatoes and onions in boiling, salted water for 15-20 minutes. Mix extract and mustard with 2 teaspoons hot water. Grate hard cheese. Drain cooked potatoes and onions and mash with the cottage cheese, salt and pepper, mustard mixture and herbs. Turn into small ovenproof dish, sprinkle with grated cheese and arrange sliced tomatoes on top. Bake for 10-15 minutes. Remove from oven and garnish with mustard and cress. Divide into 2 equal portions and serve immediately.

Makes 2 servings

Soyabean Casserole

8 oz (230 g) onion, chopped

2 cloves garlic

12 oz (340 g) canned tomatoes

2 tablespoons curry powder, or to taste

12 oz (340 g) cooked soya beans, drained weight*

1 lemon

2 tablespoons vegetable oil

salt and pepper to taste

Dry-fry chopped onions and garlic in non-stick pan for 2-3 minutes, then add tomatoes and curry powder. Cook for a further few minutes, stirring all the time. Add beans and juice of lemon. Cook for 5 minutes, stir in oil, season to taste and serve. Divide into 2 equal portions.
*Soak soya beans overnight, then cook in lightly salted water in pressure cooker for 20-25 minutes.

Makes 2 servings

Left: Cheese and Vegetable Bake
Above: Soyabean Casserole

Vegetables and Salads

Ratatouille

6 oz (170 g) aubergine	
6 oz (170 g) courgettes	
6 oz (170 g) red or green pepper	
8 oz (230 g) onion	
6 oz (170 g) green beans	
3-4 cloves garlic	
12 oz (340 g) canned tomatoes	
salt and pepper to taste	
2 tablespoons vegetable oil	

Slice aubergine and cut into cubes, slice courgettes, dice peppers and onions, slice beans, crush garlic. Place all in a large saucepan. Purée tomatoes in blender. Add to the vegetables. Season with salt and pepper, bring to boil, cover and simmer for about 30 minutes or until vegetables are soft. Just before serving, remove from heat and stir in oil. Divide into 4 equal portions. Serve at mealtime only.

Makes 4 servings

Celery and Beetroot Salad in Aspic

4 oz (110 g) canned beetroot, drained weight	
4 fl oz (110 ml) can liquid	
3 oz (80 g) celery, diced	
artificial sweetener to taste	
2 tablespoons undiluted low-calorie lime drink	
3 fl oz (80 ml) chicken stock made with $\frac{1}{2}$ cube	
1 teaspoon dried onion flakes	
1$\frac{1}{2}$ teaspoons grated horseradish	
$\frac{1}{2}$ teaspoon celery seed	
3 teaspoons unflavoured gelatine	
3 tablespoons water	
white pepper to taste	

Dice beetroot and mix with the can liquid, celery, sweetener, lime drink, stock and onion flakes. Add horseradish and celery seed. Soften gelatine in the water in a small pan. Dissolve over low heat and stir into beetroot. Season to taste with white pepper. Turn into a 1-pint mould and set in refrigerator.

Makes 1 serving

Cocktail Celery Sticks

1 lb (460 g) celery	
2 tablespoons soy sauce	
1 tablespoon vinegar	
artificial sweetener to taste	
1 teaspoon seasoning salt	

Cut celery into 1″ lengths. Blanch in boiling water for 2 minutes. Rinse in cold water, drain and cool. While still slightly warm, mix well with remaining ingredients. Chill before serving.

Makes 4–6 servings

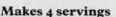

Vegetables and Salads

German Red Cabbage

12 oz (340 g) red cabbage

2 medium cooking apples

½ teaspoon ground bay leaves

¼ teaspoon cinnamon

2 tablespoons dried onion flakes

salt and pepper to taste

artificial sweetener to taste

8 teaspoons margarine

Preheat oven to 375°F, Gas Mark 5, 190°C. Wash cabbage and cut into thin strips. Peel, core and slice apples. Arrange alternate layers of apple and cabbage in a casserole. Sprinkle each layer with ground bay leaves, cinnamon, onion flakes, salt, pepper and sweetener and dot with margarine. Cover and bake in oven for 1½ hours. Divide into 4 equal portions.

Makes 4 servings

Carrot Pudding

1 lb (460 g) carrots

12 oz (340 g) peeled potatoes

salt to taste

5 fl oz (140 ml) skim milk

½ teaspoon onion powder

4 teaspoons margarine

8 oz (230 g) Cheddar cheese, grated

Peel and dice carrots. Dice potatoes. Place in large saucepan, cover with water, add salt to taste, bring to the boil and cook for 8-10 minutes, or until vegetables are tender. Strain and mash well. Add milk, onion powder and margarine, beat until thick and creamy. Add half the cheese and beat again. Turn into a heatproof dish, cover with remaining cheese and place under a hot grill until bubbly and golden. Divide into 4 equal portions. Serve at mealtime only.

Makes 4 servings

Baked Beans on Toast

For the sauce:

1½ pints (scant litre) tomato juice

2 tablespoons dried pepper flakes

1 tablespoon dried onion flakes

2–3 tablespoons cider or tarragon vinegar

2 teaspoons Worcester sauce

artificial sweetener to taste

¼ teaspoon celery salt

¼ teaspoon pepper

½ teaspoon seasoning salt

½ teaspoon tarragon flakes

12 oz (340 g) cooked haricot beans

2 slices bread (2 oz, 60 g), toasted

Combine all the sauce ingredients in a pan. Bring to the boil, stirring occasionally, and cook rapidly until reduced by a third. Allow to cool completely then purée in a blender until smooth, or press through a sieve. Return to saucepan, add the cooked haricot beans and simmer for 20 minutes. Divide evenly between toast slices and serve at once.

Makes 2 servings

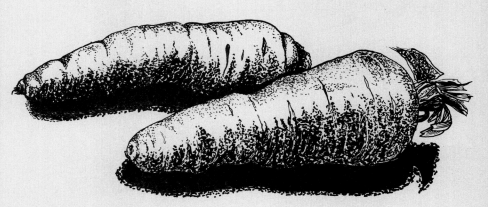

Vegetables and Salads

Celebration Salad

6 oz (170 g) red cabbage, shredded

2 tablespoons red wine vinegar

4 fl oz (110 ml) water

1 teaspoon coriander seed

1 clove garlic, finely chopped

salt and pepper to taste

1 medium eating apple

4 medium dried prunes

5 fl oz (140 ml) natural unsweetened yogurt

2 teaspoons lemon juice

artificial sweetener to taste

Place first 5 ingredients in a saucepan, season with salt and pepper, bring to boil and cook briskly for 5 minutes. Remove from heat and strain. Leave to cool. Core and chop apple, remove stones from prunes and chop. Mix with cabbage. Combine yogurt, lemon juice and sweetener. Mix thoroughly, pour over cabbage, toss to mix well. Chill lightly and divide into 2 equal portions before serving.

Makes 2 servings

Red Bean Casserole

1 lb (460 g) cooked red beans, drained weight

3 sticks celery

4 fl oz (110 ml) tomato juice

15 fl oz (430 ml) chicken stock made with 1 cube

3 oz (80 g) green pepper

4 teaspoons dried onion flakes

1 teaspoon dried basil

1 teaspoon dried marjoram

salt and pepper to taste

Preheat oven to 350°F, Gas Mark 4, 180°C. Place cooked beans in casserole with chopped celery, tomato juice, stock, green pepper, onion flakes and herbs. Season well. Bake in oven for approximately 1¼ hours. Divide into 2 equal portions and serve with green salad.

Makes 2 servings

Right: Red Bean Casserole
Below: Celebration Salad

Vegetables and Salads

Potato Cheese and Egg Bake

6 oz (170 g) cooked, peeled potatoes

2 standard eggs

2 oz (60 g) Cheddar cheese, grated

4 oz (110 g) onion, finely chopped or minced

salt and pepper to taste

Preheat oven to 375°F, Gas Mark 5, 190°C. Place cooked potato in basin and mash well with fork. Separate eggs and beat whites until stiff peaks form. Set aside. Beat egg yolks into mashed potato. Add half the cheese and half the onion, salt and pepper. Beat again thoroughly. Fold in egg whites, turn mixture into soufflé dish. Mix rest of cheese and onion together and sprinkle over top of potato. Place in oven and bake for 20-30 minutes, or until firm to touch and golden brown. Divide into 2 equal portions and serve at once.

Makes 2 servings

Fluffy Potato Casserole

12 oz (340 g) cooked, peeled potatoes

2 teaspoons dried onion flakes

1 tablespoon water

salt and pepper to taste

6 teaspoons margarine

1 oz (30 g) diced green pepper

paprika

Preheat oven to 400°F, Gas Mark 6, 200°C. Combine potatoes, onion flakes, water, salt, pepper and margarine in a mixing bowl. Beat with a wooden spoon until light and fluffy. Add diced pepper, mix well and turn into casserole. Sprinkle with paprika. Bake until top is golden brown and divide into 4 equal portions.

Makes 4 servings

Tsatsiki

10 fl oz (280 ml) natural unsweetened yogurt

6 oz (170 g) cucumber, finely diced

1 clove garlic, crushed

salt to taste

2-3 sprigs mint, chopped

paprika for garnish

Mix yogurt, cucumber, garlic, salt and mint leaves together. Chill thoroughly. Divide evenly between 4 individual dishes, sprinkle with paprika before serving.

Makes 4 servings

Vegetables and Salads

Curried Cabbage

6 oz (170 g) tomatoes

4 oz (110 g) onion, diced

12 oz (340 g) white cabbage, finely shredded

salt and pepper to taste

2 teaspoons curry powder

2 teaspoons vegetable oil

Skin and chop tomatoes and place in non-stick pan with diced onion. Cook over low heat for 2 minutes. Add finely shredded cabbage, sprinkle with salt, pepper and curry powder. Cover with lid and allow vegetables to cook in their own liquor. Shake pan frequently to prevent sticking. When cabbage is tender, but still crisp, transfer to heated dish, pour oil over and mix well. Divide into 2 equal portions and serve at once with cold or hot meat or poultry. Serve at mealtime only.

Makes 2 servings

Savoury Rice

6 oz (170 g) cooked rice

4 oz (110 g) canned pineapple tidbits, no sugar added

3 oz (80 g) green pepper

2 oz (60 g) leeks

2½ fl oz (70 ml) natural unsweetened yogurt

salt and pepper to taste

Place rice and pineapple in a bowl. Chop pepper and leeks finely and add to rice. Add yogurt, salt and pepper, mix together and chill thoroughly before serving. Divide into 2 equal portions.

Makes 2 servings

Peking Salad

4 oz (110 g) canned bamboo shoots, drained and finely shredded

6 radishes, sliced

4 teaspoons chopped watercress

3 oz (80 g) red pepper, thinly sliced

2 tablespoons cider vinegar

¼ teaspoon onion salt

½ teaspoon mixed herbs

2 tablespoons chopped parsley

salt and ground black pepper to taste

artificial sweetener to taste

Mix all ingredients well together and serve.

Makes 1 serving

Waldorf Salad

3 oz (80 g) cooked pasta shapes

1½ oz (45 g) cucumber, unpeeled

1 or 2 sticks celery

2 oz (60 g) onion

2½ fl oz (70 ml) natural unsweetened yogurt

1 tablespoon mayonnaise

garlic and celery salt to taste

1 medium red apple, unpeeled

lemon juice

Place pasta in basin. Chop cucumber, celery and onion and add to pasta. Mix yogurt with mayonnaise and seasoning, pour over pasta and vegetables. Wash and dice apple, sprinkle with lemon juice and use to decorate salad. Serve chilled.

Makes 1 serving

Salad Dressings

Tomato French Dressing

5 fl oz (140 ml) tomato juice

2 tablespoons vinegar

½–1 tablespoon Worcester sauce

salt and pepper to taste

pinch dry mustard

artificial sweetener to taste

Combine all ingredients in screw top jar and shake until well blended. Divide into 2 equal portions.

Makes 2 servings

Green Dressing

2 tablespoons mayonnaise

bunch watercress

2 tablespoons wine vinegar

1 tablespoon capers

artificial sweetener to taste

Place all ingredients in a blender and blend until smooth. Serve over green salad. Divide evenly. Serve at mealtime only.

Makes 4 servings

Salad Dressing

½ oz (15 g) nonfat dry milk

3 tablespoons water

2 tablespoons (1 oz, 30 g) tomato purée

1 teaspoon Worcester sauce

½ teaspoon prepared mustard

artificial sweetener to taste

Add milk to water, turn into blender goblet with all other ingredients and blend well. Alternatively, shake in screw top jar 2-3 minutes. Store in refrigerator.

Makes 1 serving

Cheese and Eggs

These are two very valuable foods when you're following the Weight Watchers Programme. They are so versatile that you can introduce plenty of variety into your menus, and so easy to turn into tasty dishes that you need never be tempted to skip a meal. Eggs and cheese are particularly valuable when you are eating alone – this is the time when most of us occasionally feel that we are too busy or 'can't be bothered' to cook. Set a tray attractively and make an omelette or one of our cheese and salad dishes. With a low calorie fruit drink and a colourful dessert you'll have a satisfying meal and there'll be no temptation to nibble at fattening snacks later in the day. The soft cheeses such as cottage and curd cheese are particularly useful for solitary lunchers – servings are generous and they combine perfectly with any of your favourite salads.

Cheese and Eggs

Cheese Salad with Yogurt Dressing

5 fl oz (140 ml) natural unsweetened yogurt

2 oz (60 g) spring onions, finely chopped

3 oz (80 g) cucumber, peeled and diced

salt and pepper to taste

1 small lettuce

1½ oz (45 g) green pepper

1½ oz (45 g) red pepper

6 oz (170 g) ripe tomatoes, skinned and sliced

2 oz (60 g) Cheddar cheese, diced

2 oz (60 g) Danish Blue cheese, diced

12 medium black grapes

Mix yogurt with spring onions and cucumber. Season well and keep in a cool place. Arrange lettuce on a serving dish. Remove seeds and membranes from peppers, slice peppers, mix with sliced tomatoes and season. Pile in the centre of the lettuce and top with diced cheeses and grapes. Serve with the yogurt dressing, dividing salad and dressing into 2 equal portions.

Makes 2 servings

Cheese and Vegetable Souffle

1 lb (460 g) courgettes, roughly chopped

4 oz (110 g) onion, roughly chopped

2 standard eggs, separated

2 oz (60 g) hard cheese, grated

seasoning

Preheat oven to 350°F, Gas Mark 4, 180°C. Cook courgettes and onion in a non-stick pan with 3 tablespoons water. When soft, transfer to blender with egg yolks and grated cheese. Blend until vegetables are finely chopped. Beat egg whites until stiff and fold into mixture. Pour into a small soufflé dish and bake for about 45 minutes. Divide into 2 equal portions and serve hot.

Makes 2 servings

Beetroot Burgers

8 oz (230 g) cooked beetroot, grated

8 oz (230 g) Cheddar cheese, grated

salt and pepper to taste

4 slices bread (4 oz, 110 g) toasted

Combine beetroot and cheese and season. Divide evenly into 4 and spread over toast. Place under moderate grill until golden brown. Serve with green salad.

Makes 4 servings

Cottage Cheese Crunch

1 medium eating apple, quartered and cored

1½ oz (45 g) cucumber

1½ oz (45 g) celery

1½ oz (45 g) carrot

1 oz (30 g) spring onions

3 oz (80 g) tomato

5 oz (140 g) cottage cheese

1 slice brown bread (1 oz, 30 g) toasted

Roughly chop apple, celery, cucumber, carrot and spring onions. Cut tomato into small segments. In a basin, mix all chopped ingredients with the cottage cheese. Serve chilled and garnish with toasted bread cut into small cubes.

Makes 1 serving

Golden Grill

3 oz (80 g) canned whole kernel corn, drained weight

1 oz (30 g) grated hard cheese

1 slice bread (1 oz, 30 g) toasted

3 oz (80 g) tomatoes

Heat corn and cheese gently together in a small pan until cheese melts. Place on toasted bread, cover with thin slices of tomato and grill lightly to cook tomato.

Makes 1 serving

Devilled Egg Salad

2 standard eggs, hard-boiled

2 teaspoons tomato ketchup

2 teaspoons mayonnaise

curry powder to taste

¼ teaspoon dry mustard

salt and pepper

Worcester sauce to taste

lettuce leaves

6 oz (170 g) tomatoes, quartered

Cut eggs into halves lengthwise. Carefully remove yolks and set whites aside. In a bowl, finely crumble yolks with a fork and blend in ketchup, mayonnaise, curry powder and mustard to make a smooth mixture. Season lightly. Refill egg whites with yolk mixture. Chill and serve on lettuce leaves, garnished with tomatoes.

Makes 1 serving

Cheese and Vegetable Pudding

3 oz (80 g) carrots

2 oz (60 g) onion

1 oz (30 g) Cheddar cheese

5 fl oz (140 ml) skim milk

1 slice bread (1 oz, 30 g) made into crumbs

salt and cayenne pepper

pinch dry mustard

1 standard egg

3 oz (80 g) tomato for garnish

Preheat oven to 400°F, Gas Mark 6, 200°C. Wash, scrape and thinly slice carrots. Cook in boiling, salted water for 10 minutes, drain well. Peel and thinly slice onion. Grate cheese. Pour milk into saucepan, add carrots and half the onion, simmer for a few minutes, stir in breadcrumbs and most of the cheese. Season with salt, cayenne pepper and mustard powder. Lightly beat egg and stir into milk mixture. Pour into a small ovenproof dish, top with remaining onion slices and cheese. Bake in oven until golden and well risen, approximately 30 minutes. Garnish with tomato.

Makes 1 serving

Omelette Lunch Decker

3 oz (80 g) tomatoes	
3 oz (80 g) canned mushrooms	
2 oz (60 g) peas	
5 oz (140 g) cottage cheese	
2 standard eggs	
salt and pepper to taste	
1 small lettuce	

Prepare fillings – skin and slice tomatoes, slice mushrooms, cook peas, weigh cheese. Separate eggs. Whisk whites until stiff peaks form. In a small bowl, beat egg yolks until creamy. Fold into the whites. Heat a non-stick pan and sprinkle with salt. Drop in spoonfuls of the egg mixture to form 5 miniature omelettes. Cook until top is set, turn and brown second side. Assemble sandwich: cover first omelette with peas, second with mushrooms and third with tomatoes. Spread the fourth with cheese and top with the fifth omelette. Season each layer with salt and pepper. Serve on a bed of lettuce. Divide evenly into 2 portions.

Makes 2 servings

Left: Cheese and Vegetable Pudding
Right: Omelette Lunch Decker

Cheese and Eggs

Fluffy Cheese and Onion Flan

Flan case:

1 teaspoon margarine

1 fl oz (30 ml) skim milk

2 slices bread (2 oz, 60 g) made into crumbs

Filling:

1 teaspoon margarine

2 teaspoons plain flour

2 fl oz (60 ml) skim milk

2 standard eggs, separated

4 oz (110 g) onion, chopped, cooked until soft and drained

2 oz (60 g) Cheddar cheese, grated

salt and pepper to taste

Preheat oven to 400°F, Gas Mark 6, 200°C. Make flan case: melt margarine and add skim milk. Combine with breadcrumbs. Press breadcrumb mixture onto base and sides of a 6" flan dish or tin and bake in oven for 15 minutes or until firm and lightly browned. Remove from oven. Reduce oven temperature to 350°F, Gas Mark 4, 180°C. Make filling: melt margarine in top half of double boiler, over boiling water. Stir in flour. Gradually add the milk and cook until sauce thickens, stirring occasionally. Add egg yolks, onion and most of the cheese, reserving a little for the top. Blend well, cook for 5 minutes and add seasoning to taste. Whisk egg whites until stiff and fold into cheese and onion mixture. Pile mixture into flan case, sprinkle top with remaining cheese. Bake for 25 minutes until well-risen and golden brown. Divide into 2 equal portions and serve immediately.

Makes 2 servings

Egg and Cheese Salad

2 standard eggs, hard-boiled and chopped

5 oz (140 g) cottage cheese

2 teaspoons mayonnaise

salt and pepper

lettuce leaves

3 oz (80 g) tomatoes, sliced

3 oz (80 g) carrots, grated

2 slices bread (2 oz, 60 g) toasted

Mix eggs, cottage cheese and mayonnaise together, season with salt and pepper. Arrange lettuce leaves on two plates and divide egg mixture evenly between them. Add tomatoes and grated carrots. Serve with toast.

Makes 2 servings

Macaroni Egg and Cheese

5 oz (140 g) cottage cheese

1½ fl oz (45 ml) skim milk

1 teaspoon lemon juice

6 oz (170 g) cooked macaroni

3 oz (80 g) green pepper, diced

2 standard eggs, hard-boiled and sliced

salt and pepper to taste

¼ teaspoon caraway seeds

¼ teaspoon Worcester sauce

Preheat oven to 350°F, Gas Mark 4, 180°C. Place first 3 ingredients in blender and blend until smooth. Arrange macaroni, vegetables, egg and seasonings in a small baking dish and cover with the blended mixture. Bake in oven for about 15 minutes or until thoroughly heated. Divide into 2 equal portions.

Makes 2 servings

Pear and Yogurt Mayonnaise

5 oz (140 g) cottage cheese

5 fl oz (140 ml) natural unsweetened yogurt

1 teaspoon lemon juice

artificial sweetener to taste

3 teaspoons mayonnaise

1 small ripe pear, peeled and cored

lettuce

1 teaspoon capers (optional)

3 oz (80 g) tomato

Beat together cottage cheese, yogurt, lemon juice and mayonnaise. Slice pear, place on lettuce. Spoon cottage cheese mixture over the pear, sprinkle with capers and garnish with tomato.

Makes 1 serving

Egg Spaghetti

1 standard egg

1 clove garlic, crushed

1 teaspoon dill seed

salt and pepper to taste

3 oz (80 g) hot cooked spaghetti

1 oz (30 g) hard cheese, grated

mixed green salad

parsley for garnish

Heat a heatproof serving bowl until it is hot to the touch. Break the egg into the hot bowl and beat with the garlic, dill seed, salt and pepper. Fold the piping hot spaghetti into the egg mixture. This has the effect of cooking the egg. Sprinkle with grated cheese and serve with green salad. Garnish with parsley.

Makes 1 serving

Spanish Omelette

4 oz (110 g) onion

3 oz (80 g) courgettes

1½ oz (45 g) red pepper

1½ oz (45 g) green pepper

salt and pepper

2 standard eggs

4 oz (110 g) chopped cooked turkey (or chicken)

Finely chop all vegetables. Simmer in a little salted water for 10 minutes. Drain. Beat eggs with seasoning to taste. Stir in turkey and cooked vegetables. Heat a non-stick pan, pour in mixture and cook over medium heat until lightly set. Turn carefully to brown second side or finish under a hot grill. Divide into 2 equal portions.

Makes 2 servings

Gingered Cottage Cheese

5 oz (140 g) cottage cheese

1 medium apple, peeled, sliced and stewed

½ teaspoon ground ginger

mixed green salad

Mix all ingredients lightly together in a small bowl. Cover and refrigerate until required. Serve with green salad, or as a dessert, dusted with extra ginger. This recipe is useful for using up bruised apples, and may also be used for frozen apple pieces.

Makes 1 serving.

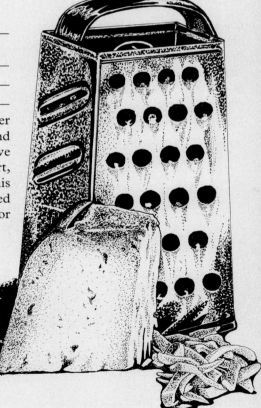

Buck Rarebit

1 slice bread (1 oz, 30 g) toasted

1 oz (30 g) Cheddar cheese, thinly sliced

curry powder to taste

1 standard egg

Cover toast completely with slices of cheese. Sprinkle with curry powder to taste. Place under medium grill until cheese is melted. Meanwhile, poach egg. Place on cooked cheese and serve at once.

Makes 1 serving

Savoury Flan

Crust:

4 slices bread (4 oz, 110 g) made into crumbs and browned in oven or under grill

5 fl oz (140 ml) natural unsweetened yogurt

salt and pepper

Filling:

4 standard eggs

5 fl oz (140 ml) natural unsweetened yogurt

4 oz (110 g) hard cheese, grated

salt and pepper to taste

6 oz (170 g) tomato

Preheat oven to 350°F, Gas Mark 4, 180°C. Mix breadcrumbs with yogurt, season with salt and pepper and press into flan ring to form flan case.
To make filling, beat eggs and yogurt together, add grated cheese, salt and pepper. Pour into flan case. Slice tomatoes and arrange in a border round the flan. Bake for 30-35 minutes or until filling is set. Divide into 4 equal portions. Serve hot or cold.

Makes 4 servings

Above: Buck Rarebit
Right: Savoury Flan

Cheese and Eggs

Mock Pizza

3 oz (80 g) green pepper

6 oz (170 g) red pepper

5 fl oz (140 ml) tomato juice

2 slices bread (2 oz, 60 g) made into crumbs

2 standard eggs

2 oz (60 g) Cheddar cheese, grated

½ teaspoon mixed dried herbs

salt and pepper to taste

3 oz (80 g) mushrooms

Remove seeds and membranes from peppers. Slice green pepper into rings and cook in boiling water for 5 minutes. Rinse in cold water and drain well. Chop red pepper and place in a saucepan with the tomato juice. Bring to the boil and simmer, uncovered, until the pepper is very soft. Mash well. Place the breadcrumbs in a non-stick frying pan and dry-fry gently until beginning to brown. Beat eggs with half the cheese, herbs, salt and pepper. Pour the eggs into the frying pan, mix with the crumbs and cook until underside is golden. Brown the top under a hot grill. Invert the pizza base carefully onto a heatproof serving dish. Spread the base with the mashed red pepper, arrange the green pepper rings and sliced mushrooms on top and sprinkle with the remaining cheese. Place under hot grill until golden brown. Divide into 2 equal portions and serve at once.

Makes 2 servings

Toastie Topper

3 oz (80 g) mushrooms

5 fl oz (140 ml) skim milk

salt and pepper to taste

1 teaspoon dried onion flakes

1 oz (30 g) cheese, grated

3 teaspoons cornflour

1 slice bread (1 oz, 30 g)

3 oz (80 g) tomatoes, sliced

Wash and chop mushrooms and place in small saucepan with milk, 1-2 tablespoons water, salt and pepper and dried onion flakes. Simmer for 10 minutes. Mix cornflour with 2 tablespoons water and add to the pan with the cheese. Stir constantly over low heat until cheese has melted and sauce has thickened. If too thick, add a little more water. Toast bread and place mixture on top. Garnish with sliced tomatoes and serve at once.

Makes 1 serving

Potato Pancakes

3 oz (80 g) cooked potato

1 slice bread (1 oz, 30 g) made into crumbs

2 standard eggs, beaten

pinch salt

1 teaspoon dried onion flakes

1 tablespoon skim milk

3 teaspoons margarine

Mash the potato. Add the breadcrumbs, eggs, salt, onion flakes and skim milk and beat well. Heat a non-stick frying pan and drop in tablespoons of the mixture. Cook until browned on both sides, turning once. Spread each cake with margarine and serve piping hot with green salad.

Makes 1 serving

French Cheese Soufflé

5 fl oz (140 ml) skim milk

2 slices bread (2 oz, 60 g) made into crumbs

2 oz (60 g) grated Cheddar cheese

salt and pepper to taste

pinch cayenne pepper

pinch dry mustard

2 standard eggs, separated

Preheat oven to 425°F, Gas Mark 7, 220°C. Heat the milk very gently in a saucepan. Add breadcrumbs, cheese, seasonings and egg yolks. Whisk egg whites until stiff and gently fold them into the cheese mixture. Pour carefully into a 6″ soufflé dish and bake in oven for about 15 minutes or until well-risen and lightly set. Divide into 2 equal portions.

Makes 2 servings

Sweet Soufflé Omelette

2 standard eggs, separated

2 tablespoons water

artificial sweetener to taste

5 oz (140 g) strawberries

2½ fl oz (70 ml) natural unsweetened yogurt

Separate eggs. In a small bowl, beat yolks with water until creamy and add sweetener. In another bowl, whisk egg whites until peaks form. Whisk a little white into yolks, then fold in remainder. Heat non-stick pan, spread egg mixture evenly over pan, cook gently until underside is brown. Place under hot grill until top is golden. Mix fruit and sweetener into yogurt. Slide omelette onto heated plate, top with yogurt mixture and fold over. Serve at once.

Makes 1 serving

Cheese and Cucumber Mousse

6 oz (170 g) cucumber

salt and white pepper to taste

2 teaspoons dried onion flakes, softened in boiling water to cover

5 oz (140 g) curd cheese

5 fl oz (140 ml) chicken stock, made with ½ cube

3 teaspoons unflavoured gelatine soaked in 3 tablespoons cold water

2 tablespoons white wine vinegar

artificial sweetener to taste

pinch ground mace

5 fl oz (140 g) natural unsweetened yogurt

mustard and cress

Dice cucumber finely, sprinkle with salt and pepper and leave to stand between 2 plates for 30 minutes. Meanwhile, drain and chop onion flakes and mix with cheese. Season with salt and pepper. Dissolve soaked gelatine in the hot stock and mix with the cheese. Drain cucumber, combine with vinegar, sweetener and mace. When cheese mixture is quite cold, fold in the cucumber and yogurt. Rinse a 1½-2 pint ring mould with cold water to prevent sticking and pour in the mousse mixture. Leave to set. Turn out and fill the centre with mustard and cress.

Makes 1 serving

Hints and Tips

Store cheese in the fridge, wrapped in food film, to prevent drying. For the finer flavoured cheeses, cut off what you need before a meal and allow it to come back to room temperature before serving.

● To achieve a hard boiled egg which will slice neatly, shake the egg gently before you slide it into the water, so that the yolk is in the middle.

● Any dry ends of hard cheeses, or crumbly bits which are past their best, may be grated or milled and stored in the fridge in a covered jar, all ready for weighing out to use in omelettes and vegetable dishes.

● Eggs will crack if you take them straight from the fridge for boiling. Try to keep a few in the kitchen ready for use. You can also minimise the risk of cracking – if you have the patience! – by making a tiny hole in the end of the egg with a needle before boiling.

Fish

You may have wondered why fish figures so largely in the Weight Watchers Programme. The simple answer is that fish is an excellent source of protein and is usually low in calories.

And fish is available in such variety that there is little risk of getting bored with it. Choosing your fish has few problems – just remember to check weights, particularly with canned or frozen fish, and to drain all the oil from canned fish before you use it. When buying fresh fish, make sure it *is* fresh – whole fish should be firm and retain their attractive colour, bright eyes and shining scales. Fillets must be firm and a good colour. Unlike many foods which tend to be the same all year round, the types of fresh fish available do still vary with the seasons and weather conditions. Be adventurous and try some of the unfamiliar ones occasionally to add zest and interest to your menus.

Fish

Herring Horizon

2 oz (60g) onion

3 oz (80 g) carrot

6 oz (170 g) fillets of fresh herring

salt and pepper to taste

6 oz (170 g) tomatoes

Cook onion in shallow flameproof pan with a little water until tender. Grate carrot, add to the pan and cook for a further 5 minutes, adding a little more water if necessary. Cut fish fillets in half lengthwise, salt and pepper well. Slice tomatoes thinly, lay slices over the onion and carrot and place the fish on top. Cover with lid or foil and cook over low heat for about 15 minutes. Serve immediately.

Makes 1 serving.

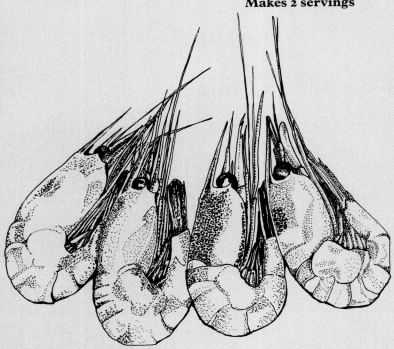

Cottage Tuna Open Sandwich

4 oz (110 g) canned tuna, drained

5 oz (140 g) cottage cheese

3 oz (80 g) tomatoes, skinned and quartered

2 oz (60 g) onion, chopped

2 tablespoons (1 oz, 30 g) tomato purée

dash Worcester sauce

2 teaspoons margarine

2 slices brown bread (2 oz, 60 g)

lettuce leaves

small piece of cucumber

Put tuna, cottage cheese, quartered tomatoes, onion, tomato purée and Worcester sauce in blender and blend until smooth. Transfer to a small basin and chill well in refrigerator. Spread bread with margarine, arrange lettuce on 2 serving plates, top with bread and divide tuna mixture evenly between the slices of bread. Cut cucumber into 'matchsticks' and use as a garnish.

Makes 2 servings

Fish Fiesta

6 oz (170 g) white fish fillet

3 fl oz (80 ml) skim milk

1 teaspoon margarine

1 teaspoon dried onion flakes

3 oz (80 g) tomatoes, sliced

3 oz (80 g) mixed green and red peppers, thinly sliced

3 oz (80 g) mushrooms, sliced

garlic salt and black pepper to taste

1 tablespoon chopped parsley

1 tablespoon lemon juice

Preheat oven to 375°F, Gas Mark 5, 190°C. Place fish in an ovenproof dish and add remaining ingredients. Bake in oven for approximately 15-20 minutes, or until vegetables are soft and fish flakes easily.

Makes 1 serving

Curried Kedgeree

6 oz (170 g) cooked rice

4 oz (110 g) cooked peas

4 oz (110 g) cooked onion

6 oz (170 g) tomatoes, chopped

12 oz (340 g) tuna, drained

1-2 teaspoons curry powder

8 fl oz (230 ml) tomato juice

salt and pepper to taste

In a large pan combine rice, peas, onions, tomatoes and tuna with 1-2 teaspoons curry powder, or to taste. Add tomato juice, salt and pepper and cook slowly for 10 minutes. Divide into 2 equal portions and serve at once.

Makes 2 servings

Bream with Piquant Stuffing

1 × 10 oz (280 g) bream

Fresh garlic or garlic salt to taste

1 tablespoon onion flakes

3 oz (80 g) green pepper, chopped

salt and pepper to taste

1 teaspoon mixed herbs

2 tablespoons vinegar

Preheat oven to 375°F, Gas Mark 5, 190°C. With a sharp knife, make shallow incisions in the sides of the fish. Rub cuts with fresh garlic or rub in garlic salt. Mix onion flakes, pepper, salt and pepper and herbs. Stuff fish with this mixture. Wrap loosely in foil, adding vinegar before sealing, and bake in oven for 30-35 minutes.

Makes 1 serving

Baked Batch

1 crusty roll (equal to 2 slices bread, 2 oz, 60 g)

4 oz (110 g) canned mackerel, drained

1 oz (30 g) mushrooms, chopped

1 oz (30 g) onion, chopped

1 teaspoon vinegar

salt and pepper to taste

Preheat oven to 375°F, Gas Mark 5, 190°C. Cut roll into two, scoop out soft centre to leave shells, make soft bread into crumbs, mix with rest of ingredients and add salt and pepper to taste. Refill roll and bake in oven for 15 minutes. Serve hot with mixed salad.

Makes 1 serving

Curried Haddock Salad

1 small head lettuce

6 oz (170 g) cooked cod or haddock

1 medium eating apple, grated

2 slices canned pineapple, no sugar added, with 2 tablespoons juice

2 oz (60 g) onion, finely chopped

1 teaspoon curry powder, or to taste

salt and pepper to taste

1 tablespoon mayonnaise

2 oz (60 g) cooked peas

3 oz (80 g) tomato

Wash the lettuce and arrange round the edge of a plate. Flake the fish and arrange on the lettuce leaves. Combine grated apple, chopped pineapple and juice, chopped onion, curry powder, seasoning and mayonnaise. Spoon the mixture over the fish. Garnish with peas and sliced tomato and serve.

Makes 1 serving

Baked Mackerel with Cucumber Stuffing

1 oz (30 g) onion, chopped

1½ oz (45 g) cucumber, diced

1 slice bread (1 oz, 30 g) made into crumbs

1 tablespoon chopped parsley

2 tablespoons lemon juice

salt and pepper

1 × 10 oz (280 g) mackerel

Preheat oven to 375°F, Gas Mark 5, 190°C. Simmer onion and cucumber in a little water for 5 minutes. Drain and mix with breadcrumbs, parsley, lemon and seasoning. Stuff the mackerel and place in an ovenproof dish lined with foil. Cover and bake for 30 minutes.

Makes 1 serving

Tuna Surprise

3 teaspoons margarine

3 teaspoons cornflour

5 fl oz (140 ml) skim milk

salt and pepper to taste

pinch dry mustard

1 oz (30 g) grated hard cheese

3 oz (80 g) cooked rice

2 oz (60 g) cooked peas

3 oz (80 g) cooked diced carrots

2 oz (60 g) canned tuna, drained

1 slice white bread (1 oz, 30 g), made into crumbs

Preheat oven to 400°F, Gas Mark 6, 200°C. Melt margarine in top half of double boiler over boiling water and stir in cornflour. Blend in milk and cook, stirring, until sauce thickens. Add salt and pepper to taste. Remove pan from heat, stir in mustard and cheese. Add rice, vegetables and tuna and mix well. Pour into ovenproof dish and top with breadcrumbs. Bake in oven for 25 minutes until hot through and brown.

Makes 1 serving

Hints and Tips

Buy fresh fish on the day it is to be eaten whenever possible. If it is in really prime condition it may be kept for 24 hours in the fridge, wrapped in food film and stored on cracked ice.

● Lemon and fish have an affinity. Sprinkle the juice over fish before grilling, use lemon slices and wedges as a garnish.

Baked Fish Delight

12 oz (340 g) white fish fillet

lemon juice

4 oz (110 g) peeled shrimps

2 teaspoons chives, finely chopped

2 teaspoons parsley, finely chopped

6 oz (170 g) tomatoes

salt and pepper to taste

2 tablespoons skim milk

Preheat oven to 375°F, Gas Mark 5, 190°C. Place fish in small ovenproof dish lined with foil. Sprinkle with lemon juice. Put peeled shrimps on top and sprinkle with chives and parsley. Cut tomatoes and place round edges. Season to taste. Pour skim milk over fish. Draw foil together and bake in oven for 20 minutes. Serve with salad. Divide evenly into 2 portions before serving.

Makes 2 servings

Prawns with Tomatoes

1 oz (30 g) onion

1 clove garlic

6 oz (170 g) tomatoes

salt and pepper to taste

3 oz (80 g) hot cooked rice

6 oz (170 g) peeled prawns

Chop onion finely and dry-fry gently. Crush the clove of garlic with a little salt and chop. Add to onion. Skin and de-seed tomatoes and chop into small pieces, add to onions and cook gently. Adjust seasoning. Remove from heat. Arrange hot rice on serving dish, pour over tomato mixture, decorate with prawns and serve.

Makes 1 serving

Left: Baked Fish Delight
Above: Prawns with Tomato

Fish

Tuna Mac Salad

6 oz (170 g) cooked macaroni

8 oz (230 g) canned tuna, drained and flaked

2 tablespoons mayonnaise

2 teaspoons chopped parsley

3 oz (80 g) cucumber, finely chopped

2 oz (60 g) onion, chopped

salt and pepper to taste

seasoning salt (optional)

$\frac{1}{4}$ teaspoon celery seed

2 teaspoons lemon juice

Chop macaroni and add flaked tuna. Add all remaining ingredients and mix well. Transfer to a bowl, cover, chill in refrigerator for 2-3 hours. Divide into 2 equal portions and serve with lettuce and tomatoes.

Makes 2 servings

Fresh Mackerel Pâté

1 × 10 oz (280 g) mackerel

2 slices lemon

1 teaspoon mixed herbs

1 slice bread (1 oz, 30 g) made into crumbs

1 tablespoon fish liquor

1 teaspoon low-calorie salad dressing

1½ tablespoon lemon juice

1 teaspoon margarine

1 tablespoon chopped parsley

1 slice lemon for garnish

sprigs of parsley for garnish

Preheat oven to 400°F, Gas Mark 6, 200°C. Wrap fish loosely in foil with the lemon slices and herbs. Bake in oven for 30 minutes. When cooked, unwrap foil, remove herbs and lemon, drain and reserve the juices. Remove skin and bones from fish and mash fish with the breadcrumbs, adding the cooking liquor, salad dressing, lemon juice and margarine. Beat together. Season to taste and add parsley. Press into a small dish and decorate with slice of lemon and sprigs of parsley. Chill in refrigerator until required.

Makes 1 serving

Fish Special

12 oz (340 g) plaice fillets, skinned

1 teaspoon salt

1 tablespoon lemon juice

4 tablespoons (2 oz, 60 g) tomato purée

1 tablespoon white wine vinegar

1 teaspoon grated horseradish

3 oz (80 g) cucumber, diced

4 oz (110 g) onion, diced

2 slices bread (2 oz, 60 g) made into crumbs

1 lemon, sliced

parsley for garnish

tomato for garnish

Preheat oven to 400°F, Gas Mark 6, 200°C. Put plaice in a dish and sprinkle with salt and lemon juice. Leave for 15 minutes. Mix together tomato purée, vinegar, horseradish and cucumber and onions. Transfer half the fish to a baking dish, cover with half the vegetable mixture and the rest of the fish. Top with remaining vegetable mixture. Cover with breadcrumbs and bake in oven for 25 minutes. Arrange twists of lemon round the fish and garnish with sprigs of parsley and slices of tomato. Divide into 2 equal portions.

Makes 2 servings

Fish Patties with Sauce Delicious

2 oz (60 g) canned fish, drained

1 slice bread (1 oz, 30 g), made into crumbs

1 standard egg, beaten

2 teaspoons dried onion flakes

1 tablespoon chopped parsley

salt and pepper to taste

For the sauce:

2 teaspoons mayonnaise

2 teaspoons tomato ketchup

1 teaspoon dried onion flakes

1 oz (30 g) pickled cucumber, chopped

Mix together all ingredients for the patties. Chill in refrigerator for 10 minutes. Form into two patties and cook in non-stick pan until golden brown on both sides. Mix all sauce ingredients together. Serve the patties hot or cold, accompanied by the sauce and a mixed salad.

Makes 1 serving

Fish Mayonnaise

1½ lb (700 g) cod fillets

salt and pepper to taste

8 oz (230 g) peeled prawns

1 lb (460 g) cucumber, peeled and diced

4 tablespoons mayonnaise

chopped chives for garnish

Poach cod in water seasoned with salt and pepper. When fish flakes easily with a fork, lift out carefully with a fish slice. Remove skin and any remaining bones, flake fish into bowl, add prawns and cucumber. Add mayonnaise and mix carefully. Divide evenly between 4 plates and serve garnished with chives.

Makes 4 servings

Fish Soufflé

2 standard eggs, separated

salt and pepper to taste

1 tablespoon lemon juice

1 teaspoon Worcester sauce or to taste

2 slices white bread (2 oz, 60 g) made into crumbs

4 oz (110 g) onion, minced

6 oz (170 g) minced raw fish, without skin or bone

4 slices lemon for garnish

Preheat oven to 375°F, Gas Mark 5, 190°C. Beat egg yolks with salt, pepper, lemon juice and Worcester sauce. Gradually add the breadcrumbs and minced onion. Beat whites until stiff. Gently fold the minced fish and the yolk mixture into the beaten whites. Turn into a soufflé dish or casserole and bake for 1 hour. Serve garnished with lemon. Divide into 2 equal portions.

Makes 2 servings

Hot Spicy Fish

6 fl oz (170 ml) tomato juice

black pepper to taste

1 teaspoon Worcester sauce

1 teaspoon mixed herbs

1 teaspoon dried or fresh mint

8 oz (230 g) cod fillet

6 oz (170 g) cucumber, sliced

Preheat oven to 400°F, Gas Mark 6, 200°C. Mix together tomato juice, black pepper, Worcester sauce, herbs and mint. Pour over fish and bake in oven for 15-20 minutes. Arrange cucumber round the fish and cook for a further 5-10 minutes. Serve at once.

Makes 1 serving

Haddock or Cod Poached in Lettuce

4 large lettuce leaves

4 × 6 oz (170 g) fillets of haddock or cod

salt and pepper to taste

1 teaspoon mixed herbs

juice and grated rind of 1 lemon

5 fl oz (140 ml) skim milk

2 teaspoons cornflour

3 oz (80 g) mushrooms, sliced

Preheat oven to 375°F, Gas Mark 5, 190°C. Wash and dry lettuce leaves. Wash and skin the fish, wrap each piece in a lettuce leaf and place in a small ovenproof dish. Sprinkle seasoning and herbs over and add lemon rind and juice and 3-4 tablespoons water. Cover and bake in oven for about 20-25 minutes. Drain off liquid and keep fish hot. Blend milk with cornflour and stir into liquid. Bring to boil, stirring until thickened. Stir in sliced mushrooms and cook for 2 minutes. Pour over fish, divide into 4 equal portions and serve at once.

Makes 4 servings

Tuna Fish Cocktail

8 oz (230 g) canned tuna, drained

1 oz (30 g) onion, chopped

1 teaspoon lemon juice

2 tablespoons mayonnaise

2 tablespoons (1 oz, 30 g) tomato purée

pepper to taste

4-6 lettuce leaves

2-3 sprigs parsley

pinch paprika

4 slices lemon for garnish

3 oz (80 g) tomato for garnish

Break tuna into pieces. Mix onion, lemon juice, mayonnaise and tomato purée and season with pepper. Add tuna and mix gently. Shred lettuce and arrange in 4 glasses. Divide fish mixture evenly between the glasses and add parsley sprigs and a dusting of paprika. Garnish with slices of lemon and tomato on the rim of the glasses.

Makes 4 servings

Baked Cod Steaks

2 tablespoons lemon juice

½ teaspoon salt

½ teaspoon paprika

4 × 8 oz (230 g) cod steaks

4 oz (110 g) onion, chopped

6 oz (170 g) green pepper, cut into strips

1 lemon cut in wedges

Preheat oven to 425°F, Gas Mark 7, 220°C. Combine lemon juice, salt and paprika. Pour into a shallow ovenproof dish. Add fish and leave to marinate for 1 hour, turning once. Cook onions in non-stick pan with a little water until soft. Drain. Arrange strips of green pepper over cod steaks, sprinkle onions over fish. Bake uncovered in oven for 15 minutes or until fish flakes. Serve with lemon wedges.

Makes 4 servings

Above: Tuna Fish Cocktail
Right: Baked Cod Steaks

Fish

Tunny Peps

2 × 6 oz (170 g) green peppers

4 oz (110 g) onion, chopped

2 cloves garlic, crushed

6 oz (170 g) canned tomatoes, drained weight

2 tablespoons (1 oz, 30 g) tomato purée

$\frac{1}{4}$ teaspoon dried basil

$\frac{1}{4}$ teaspoon dried oregano

salt and black pepper to taste

1 tablespoon chopped parsley

2 teaspoons capers

8 oz (230 g) canned tuna, drained

Preheat oven to 400°F, Gas Mark 6, 200°C. Cut tops off peppers to a depth of about 1″. Remove stems from the tops, chop the flesh and set aside. Scrape pith and seeds from pepper 'cups'. Mix together all remaining ingredients except tuna, cook in saucepan over moderate heat until thick. Add flaked tuna and chopped pepper. Fill pepper 'cups' with sauce, reserving any remaining sauce. Bake in oven in covered dish for 35 minutes. Remove cover, top the peppers with remaining sauce and bake for a further 10 minutes.

Makes 2 servings

Kipper Kedgeree

4 oz (110 g) kipper fillets

2$\frac{1}{2}$ fl oz (70 ml) natural unsweetened yogurt

1 teaspoon lemon juice

6 oz (170 g) hot cooked rice

salt and pepper to taste

2 standard eggs, hard-boiled

parsley for garnish

Place kipper in a shallow pan of water, bring to the boil and poach gently for 2 minutes. Drain fish and flake, removing any skin. Mix with yogurt, lemon juice, rice and seasonings and transfer to serving dish. Finely chop eggs and sprinkle over the kipper mixture. Garnish with finely chopped parsley. Divide into 2 equal portions before serving.

Makes 2 servings

Kipper Cocktail

6 oz (170 g) canned kipper fillets, drained

4 fl oz (110 ml) orange juice

2 sticks celery, chopped

pepper to taste

1 small lettuce, shredded

1 lemon, sliced

Skin kipper fillets and cut into slices. Mix them with orange juice and celery. Season well with pepper and divide mixture evenly between 2 individual sundae glasses on a bed of shredded lettuce. Garnish with lemon slices.

Makes 2 servings

Pickled Fish

8 oz (230 g) coley fillet

2 oz (60 g) onion

4 tablespoons cider vinegar

2 tablespoons water

1 teaspoon curry powder

salt and pepper to taste

artificial sweetener to taste

Grill fish, skin side up, for 3-4 minutes, according to thickness. Turn and grill a further 3-4 minutes. Remove skin and any remaining bones. Transfer to a shallow dish. Meanwhile slice onion into a small saucepan, add vinegar, water, curry powder, seasoning and sweetener. Bring to the boil and cook until soft but still crisp, about 5-6 minutes. Pour onion mixture over the fish. Chill well and serve with mixed salad.

Makes 1 serving

Kipper Pâté

6 oz (170 g) canned kipper fillets, drained

1 oz (30 g) nonfat dry milk

2 tablespoons water

4 teaspoons margarine

cayenne pepper to taste

1 tablespoon lemon juice

$\frac{1}{4}$ teaspoon powdered mace (optional)

lemon and cucumber slices for garnish

Place all ingredients in a bowl and mash or pound well until they form a paste. Transfer to a small dish, garnish with lemon and cucumber. Chill well. Divide into 2 equal portions and serve with green salad.

Makes 2 servings

Mackerel Stuffed Eggs in Curry Sauce

2 standard eggs, hard-boiled

4 oz (110 g) canned mackerel, drained

4 teaspoons mayonnaise

2 teaspoons lemon juice

garlic salt and pepper to taste

6 oz (170 g) hot, cooked rice

For the sauce:

10 fl oz (280 ml) water

6 tablespoons (3 oz, 80 g) tomato purée

1 chicken stock cube

4 teaspoons onion flakes

artificial sweetener to taste

garlic salt to taste

2 teaspoons curry powder

Preheat oven to 400°F, Gas Mark 6, 200°C. Slice eggs in half lengthwise. Take out yolks, put yolks in basin with mackerel, mayonnaise, lemon juice, garlic salt and pepper and mix thoroughly. Place halved egg whites in ovenproof casserole, divide mackerel mixture equally between them. Combine sauce ingredients and simmer for 10 minutes. Pour over the eggs and bake in oven for 15 minutes. Divide eggs, sauce and rice into 2 equal portions before serving.

Makes 2 servings

Trout with Orange

1 pint (570 ml) water

2 bay leaves

salt and pepper to taste

2 × 10 oz (280 g) trout

8 fl oz (230 ml) orange juice

4 tablespoons lemon juice

4 teaspoons cornflour

2 tablespoons margarine

2 tablespoons chopped parsley

1 lemon, sliced

Bring water to boil in large saucepan with bay leaves, salt and pepper. Gently poach trout for 15 minutes, remove and keep hot. In a small pan, mix 10 fl oz (280 ml) of the cooking liquid with the orange and lemon juice. Blend the cornflour with a little cold water and add to the pan. Bring to the boil and simmer gently until thickened. Remove from heat and beat in margarine and parsley. Pour sauce over trout and garnish with parsley and lemon slices. Divide into 2 equal portions before serving.

Makes 2 servings

Seafood Special

1 lettuce, shredded

4 oz (110 g) peeled prawns

2 oz (60 g) shelled cockles

2 oz (60 g) shelled mussels

2 oz (60 g) button mushrooms, sliced

6 oz (170 g) tomatoes

4 oz (110 g) cooked peas

2 tablespoons mayonnaise

1 tablespoon vinegar

1 teaspoon prepared mustard

dash Worcester sauce

1 tablespoon ($\frac{1}{2}$ oz, 15 g) tomato purée

Arrange lettuce in 2 individual dishes. Divide mixed fish evenly between the dishes. Cover with button mushrooms, tomatoes and peas. Mix together mayonnaise, vinegar, mustard, Worcester sauce and tomato purée. Pour over fish mixture; chill thoroughly before serving.

Makes 2 servings

Cheesy Fish Grill

1 slice bread (1 oz, 30 g)

1½ oz (45 g) cooked smoked fish

1 oz (30 g) onion, finely sliced

3 oz (80 g) tomato, sliced

salt and pepper to taste

1 oz (30 g) cheese, grated

Toast bread on one side. Place fish on untoasted side. Cover fish with onion and season with salt and pepper. Top with tomato and cheese. Grill slowly until cheese is melted. Serve with green salad.

Makes 1 serving

Fish Pudding

2 slices bread (2 oz, 60 g) made into crumbs

5 fl oz (140 ml) skim milk

4 oz (110 g) canned salmon, drained

2 standard eggs, beaten

1 tablespoon lemon juice

salt and pepper to taste

Preheat oven to 350°F, Gas Mark 4, 180°C. Soak breadcrumbs in milk. Remove dark skin and bones from salmon and mash the fish. Add to breadcrumbs and milk. Add beaten eggs, lemon juice, salt and pepper. Mix well, pour into an ovenproof dish or soufflé dish and bake for 35 minutes. Divide into 2 equal portions and serve hot or cold with green beans or salad.

Makes 2 servings

Above: Cheesy Fish Grill
Right: Fish Pudding

Fish

Quick and Easy Shrimp Chow Mein

3 oz (80 g) celery, diced

4 fl oz (110 ml) chicken stock made with ½ cube

1 oz (30 g) onion, chopped

1 tablespoon soy sauce

3 oz (80 g) canned bamboo shoots, drained and chopped

3 oz (80 g) canned bean sprouts, drained

6 oz (170 g) peeled shrimps

3 oz (80 g) fresh mushrooms, sliced

Put half the celery and stock in blender. Blend until smooth. Pour into saucepan, add onion, soy sauce, bamboo shoots, bean sprouts and remainder of celery. Simmer for 10 minutes. Add shrimps. Lightly brown mushrooms in non-stick pan, fold into mixture. Heat thoroughly and serve.

Makes 1 serving

Sardine and Tomato Toast

1 slice bread (1 oz, 30 g)

2 oz (60 g) sardines, drained

3 oz (80 g) tomato

salt and pepper to taste

1 oz (30 g) Cheddar cheese, grated

cayenne pepper to taste

watercress for garnish

Toast bread and lay sardines on top. Peel and slice tomato very thinly and place on top of sardines. Season and sprinkle with the cheese. Cook under a hot grill until cheese is bubbly and golden. Sprinkle with cayenne pepper and garnish with watercress. Serve at once.

Makes 1 serving

Cheddar Cod

1 oz (30 g) Cheddar cheese, grated

1 tablespoon skim milk

1 teaspoon French mustard

salt and pepper to taste

3 oz (80 g) cod fillet

1 teaspoon lemon juice

Preheat grill to medium. Mix cheese and milk in a bowl, add mustard, salt and pepper. Line grill pan with foil or use a heatproof dish. Sprinkle fish with lemon juice, place in the pan and grill for 5 minutes. Turn and grill second side for 5 minutes. Take fish from grill and spread with cheese mix. Return to grill and cook for a further 3 minutes or until golden brown.

Makes 1 serving

Pilchard Charlotte

4 oz (110 g) canned pilchards, drained

3 oz (80 g) cooked potato

2 fl oz (60 ml) skim milk

salt and pepper to taste

1 slice bread (1 oz, 30 g) made into crumbs

2 oz (60 g) tomatoes, peeled and sliced

3 teaspoons margarine

Preheat oven to 375°F, Gas Mark 5, 190°C. Flake fish in basin, mix with potato, milk and seasoning. Transfer to shallow ovenproof dish, sprinkle with breadcrumbs and arrange tomato slices on top. Dot with margarine and bake in oven for 30 minutes or until top is golden brown.

Makes 1 serving

Mackerel in Yogurt

2 × 10 oz (280 g) mackerel

1 teaspoon dried herbs

salt and pepper to taste

6 oz (170 g) cucumber

wine vinegar

2 oz (60 g) onion

10 fl oz (280 ml) natural unsweetened yogurt

chopped parsley

paprika

Sprinkle mackerel inside and out with herbs, salt and pepper. Place under a hot grill and cook for about 5 minutes each side. Remove from grill and leave to cool. Slice cucumber thinly, cut each slice into quarters, cover with wine vinegar and leave for 2 hours. Slice onions thinly into rings and separate. Season yogurt with salt and pepper to taste. In a serving dish arrange a layer of cucumber and onion slices, cover with a layer of yogurt. Next arrange a layer of mackerel, skinned, boned and broken into pieces. Cover with another layer of yogurt. Continue until ingredients are used up, finishing with a layer of yogurt and retaining some of the cucumber to arrange round the sides of the dish. Garnish with chopped parsley and paprika. Serve well chilled. Divide into 2 equal portions before serving.

Makes 2 servings

Right: Mackerel in Yogurt

Fish

Haddock and Sweetcorn in Cheese Sauce

12 oz (340 g) haddock fillet

12 oz (340 g) canned whole kernel sweetcorn

10 fl oz (280 ml) skim milk

4 teaspoons flour

4 teaspoons margarine

salt and pepper to taste

4 oz (110 g) Swiss cheese, grated

1 tablespoon chopped chives

Poach haddock in salted water for 3-4 minutes, or until it flakes easily. Lift out with fish slice. Remove skin and any remaining bones. Flake fish with a fork. Place sweetcorn in a 2-pint heatproof dish and cover with flaked fish. Blend milk, flour and margarine in blender. Pour into top of double saucepan over boiling water, season with salt and pepper to taste and cook until mixture thickens. Pour over fish. Mix cheese and chives and spread over fish. Place under hot grill until bubbly and golden. Divide into 4 equal portions and serve with green salad.

Makes 4 servings

Coquilles St. Jacques

6 oz (170 g) fresh or frozen scallops

3 oz (80 g) button mushrooms, sliced

6 fl oz (170 ml) skim milk

1 tablespoon chopped parsley

pinch garlic powder

salt and pepper to taste

3 teaspoons cornflour

2 oz (60 g) grated hard cheese

6 oz (170 g) hot cooked potato

3 tablespoons skim milk

4 teaspoons margarine

Preheat oven to 400°F, Gas Mark 6, 200°C. Slice scallops and place in saucepan with mushrooms, milk, parsley, garlic powder and seasoning to taste. Bring to the boil over medium heat and simmer gently for 5 minutes. Mix cornflour to a paste with a little water, add to scallop mixture and cook until thickened. Stir in half the cheese. Beat potato with skim milk, margarine and seasoning. Divide potato evenly and make a border round 2 scallop shells or small ovenproof dishes. Divide scallop mixture evenly between the shells. Sprinkle each with half the remaining cheese and bake for approximately 20 minutes.

Makes 2 servings

Skate with Orange

1 tablespoon salt

1¾ pints (1 litre) water

3 tablespoons wine vinegar

1 sachet bouquet garni

6 peppercorns

2 × 10 oz (280 g) wings of skate

4 oz (110 g) onion, sliced

1 medium orange

2 fl oz (60 ml) undiluted low-calorie orange drink

1 teaspoon wine vinegar

salt and black pepper to taste

1 teaspoon chopped parsley

1 teaspoon dried thyme

watercress for garnish

Prepare a *court bouillon* by dissolving the salt in the water in a large saucepan. Add the vinegar, *bouquet garni* and peppercorns. Bring to the boil and boil for 5 minutes. Leave to cool. Cut the skate into 4 pieces and place it in a large saucepan. Strain the *court bouillon* onto the fish. Bring slowly to boiling point, cover the pan and simmer for about 10 minutes. Meanwhile prepare sauce. Dry-fry the sliced onion gently in a non-stick pan until soft. Peel the orange and cut into ¼″ slices. Add the orange drink, vinegar, seasoning and herbs to the cooked onion. Bring to the boil, add the orange slices and simmer gently. Arrange the cooked skate in a heated serving dish. Pour the prepared sauce over the fish and garnish with sprigs of watercress. Divide into 2 equal portions.

Makes 2 Servings

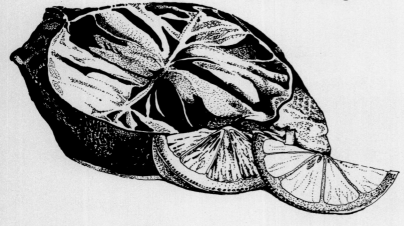

Sauces for Fish

Torange Dressing

4 fl oz (110 ml) tomato juice

1 tablespoon vegetable oil

pinch salt

pinch black pepper

grated rind and juice of 1 medium orange

1 teaspoon Worcester sauce

1 teaspoon soy sauce

1 teaspoon dried onion flakes

Shake all ingredients together in a screw top jar. Best made 3-4 hours before use. Delicious with fish.

Makes 1 serving

Sweet and Sour Sauce

5 fl oz (140 ml) water

2 fl oz (60 ml) cider vinegar

1 fl oz (30 ml) lemon juice

1 fl oz (30 ml) soy sauce

4 teaspoons tomato ketchup

pinch pepper

1 stock cube

artificial sweetener to taste

1 tablespoon dried onion flakes

3 teaspoons cornflour

3 oz (80 g) green pepper, diced

Put water, vinegar, lemon juice, soy sauce, ketchup, pepper, stock cube sweetener and onion flakes in small saucepan. Bring to boil and simmer until onion flakes are soft. Add cornflour, mixed with a little water. Add diced peppers, bring to the boil stirring constantly, and cook for 2 minutes. Serve either hot or cold with fish, meat or poultry. Divide evenly.

Makes 2 servings

Parsley Sauce

4 teaspoons flour

10 fl (280 ml) skim milk

2 tablespoons chopped parsley

salt and pepper to taste

3 teaspoons margarine

In a cup mix flour with a little of the skim milk. Put the remaining milk into a saucepan with the parsley, salt and pepper and stir in the flour mixture. Bring gradually to the boil and cook, stirring all the time, for 3 minutes. Remove from heat, add margarine and mix until well blended. Serve with fish, poultry or ham. Divide evenly.

Makes 2 servings.

Tomato Sauce

3 oz (80 g) tomato purée

6 fl oz (170 ml) water

$\frac{1}{8}$ teaspoon ground cloves

1 teaspoon basil flakes

1 tablespoon lemon juice

artificial sweetener to taste

$\frac{1}{2}$ teaspoon chilli seasoning

$\frac{1}{4}$ teaspoon garlic salt

pinch pepper

Combine all ingredients in a saucepan, bring to boil and simmer for 3 minutes. Divide evenly.

Makes 4 servings

Tangy Yogurt Sauce

5 fl oz (140 ml) natural unsweetened yogurt

4 teaspoons tomato ketchup

1 tablespoon Worcester sauce

1 tablespoon lemon juice

1 tablespoon mayonnaise

$\frac{1}{2}$ teaspoon grated horseradish

Mix all ingredients together. Chill. Use for prawn cocktail, or serve with tuna or other fish. Divide into 2 equal portions.

Makes 2 servings

Hints and Tips

● Use kitchen foil whenever you can. Fish cooked in 'parcels' with herbs and seasoning means no smell and no washing up! Have the foil big enough to leave air space in the parcel, and use the juices to make your sauce.

● Herbs which marry well with fish include parsley, bay leaves and fennel. Try baking fish with stalks of fresh fennel in the summer, keep dried bay leaves and fennel seeds for the winter.

● To give extra flavour to poached fish, simmer herbs, peppercorns, a carrot and a few onion flakes in water for an hour. Strain into a clean pan, add the fish and poach in the usual way.

● There are several ways of cooking kippers, but the simplest is to put them skin side up in a large pan and cover them with hot water. Bring to the boil, cover, turn off the heat and leave for 4-5 minutes or until the flesh flakes easily. If you have a big enough jug you can stand the kippers in this and fill it up with boiling water.

Meat

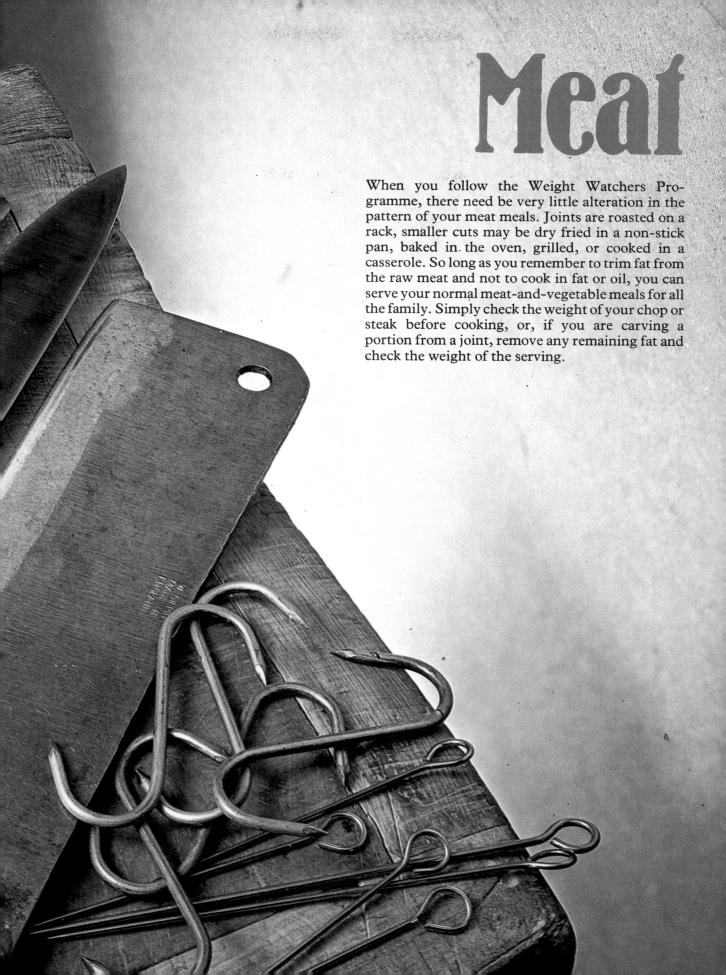

When you follow the Weight Watchers Programme, there need be very little alteration in the pattern of your meat meals. Joints are roasted on a rack, smaller cuts may be dry fried in a non-stick pan, baked in the oven, grilled, or cooked in a casserole. So long as you remember to trim fat from the raw meat and not to cook in fat or oil, you can serve your normal meat-and-vegetable meals for all the family. Simply check the weight of your chop or steak before cooking, or, if you are carving a portion from a joint, remove any remaining fat and check the weight of the serving.

Lamb

Persian Spiced Lamb

1 tablespoon dried onion flakes

2 cloves garlic

3 oz (80 g) tomatoes

12 oz (340 g) cooked lamb

¼ teaspoon ground allspice

¼ teaspoon ground mace

¼ teaspoon ground coriander

¼ teaspoon ground cinnamon

¼ teaspoon ground ginger

¼ teaspoon pepper

¼ teaspoon salt

4 fl oz (110 ml) chicken stock made with ½ cube

1 medium dessert apple, cored and chopped into small pieces

½ teaspoon powdered turmeric

6 oz (170 g) hot cooked rice

1 lemon

Place the onion flakes in a non-stick pan with crushed garlic, roughly chopped tomatoes and the meat cut into small cubes. Mix the spices and stir into the meat. Add chicken stock, heat gently and simmer for 15 minutes. Add the apple. Fork the turmeric powder into the cooked rice until evenly coloured and transfer to a serving dish. Heap the lamb in the centre and serve with lemon slices. Divide into 2 equal portions.

Makes 2 servings

Lamb Curry

4 oz (110 g) onion, finely sliced

6 oz (170 g) carrots, sliced

1½ pints (scant litre) chicken stock made with 1 cube

artificial sweetener to taste

3 tablespoons lemon juice

2 teaspoons curry powder (or to taste)

1 bay leaf (optional)

salt and pepper to taste

1 lb (460 g) lean cooked lamb, cubed

12 oz (340 g) hot cooked rice

4 oz (110 g) onion rings

6 oz (170 g) tomatoes, quartered

2 bananas

Dry-fry the sliced onion until lightly browned in a thick-based saucepan. Add the carrots, chicken stock, artificial sweetener, 2 tablespoons lemon juice, curry powder, bay leaf, salt and pepper. Bring to the boil and simmer until vegetables are soft, approximately 30 minutes. Add the lamb and cook for a further 20 minutes. Serve with the rice and side dishes of onion rings, tomato quarters and bananas sliced and sprinkled with 1 tablespoon lemon juice. Divide into 4 equal portions.

Makes 4 servings

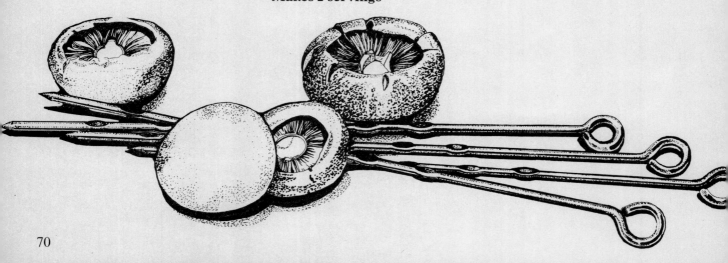

Lamb in Mint Jelly

3 oz (80 g) carrots, diced

2 oz (60 g) peas

2 oz (60 g) onion, chopped

6-8 sprigs fresh mint

10 fl oz (280 ml) stock made with 1 chicken stock cube

2 teaspoons unflavoured gelatine

6 oz (170 g) cold cooked lamb, diced

Simmer carrots, peas, onions and mint together in stock for approximately 15 minutes. Strain. Dissolve gelatine in 1 tablespoon warm water, add to stock and allow to cool. As the jelly begins to thicken, add diced meat, pour into a small tin or mould and allow to set. Turn out and serve with mixed salad.

Makes 1 serving

Shepherd's Pie

6 oz (170 g) minced cooked lamb

4 fl oz (110 ml) tomato juice

4 tablespoons beef stock made with ½ cube

4 oz (110 g) cooked, chopped onion

3 oz (80 g) cooked, chopped carrots

salt and pepper to taste

1 teaspoon dried mixed herbs

3 oz (80 g) cooked potato

paprika

Preheat oven to 400°F, Gas Mark 6, 200°C. Place the lamb in a saucepan with the tomato juice, stock, vegetables, salt and pepper and mixed herbs. Bring to the boil, stirring, cover pan and simmer for 15 minutes. Spoon the meat mixture into an ovenproof dish. Mash the cooked potato and place on top of the meat. Sprinkle with a little paprika. Bake in oven for 15 minutes, or until top is golden brown.

Makes 1 serving

Spicy Casserole

1 lb 2 oz (520 g) cooked lamb

2 teaspoons dry mustard

4 fl oz (110 ml) chicken stock made with ½ cube

½ teaspoon dried mixed herbs

1 medium cooking apple

1 lemon

4 fl oz (110 ml) orange juice

artificial sweetener to taste

½ teaspoon paprika

Preheat oven to 375°F, Gas Mark 5, 190°C. Cut the lamb into 1″ cubes. Place the meat in a shallow casserole. Stir the mustard into the stock, add herbs and pour over meat. Peel, core and slice apple into thick rings and place them on top of the meat. Sprinkle with the grated rind and juice of the lemon, add orange juice and artificial sweetener. Sprinkle with paprika. Cover and bake in oven for about 35 minutes. Divide into 3 equal portions.

Makes 3 servings

Lamb

Coriander Lamb

1 large clove garlic

2 tablespoons coriander seeds

salt and pepper to taste

4 × 10 oz (280 g) slices of lamb from top of leg

Peel garlic, crush with the coriander seeds and mix thoroughly with salt and pepper. Press the mixture onto both sides of the slices of lamb and leave in a cool place for at least 1 hour. Grill on a rack under a moderate grill, turning once during cooking. Allow approximately 6 minutes each side or grill until meat is cooked through and both sides are crisp and brown. Serve with salad.

Makes 4 servings

Lamb Kebabs

1 lb (460 g) boneless lamb, cut into cubes

5 fl oz (140 ml) natural unsweetened yogurt

juice of 1 lemon

6 oz (170 g) small tomatoes, halved

6 oz (170 g) large button mushrooms

6 oz (170 g) green peppers, deseeded and blanched for 1 minute, cut into 8 pieces

2 sticks celery, washed and blanched for 1 minute, cut into pieces

4 oz (110 g) small whole onions, peeled and blanched

garlic salt to taste

Marinate cubed lamb in yogurt and lemon juice for 6-8 hours, or overnight. Preheat oven to 375°F, Gas Mark 5, 190°C. Thread 2 kebab skewers with alternating pieces of meat and vegetables, reserving the remaining marinade. Season completed kebabs with garlic salt. Arrange skewers on a rack in a baking tin and cook in the oven for about 30 minutes. Turn reserved marinade into a small pan and reheat gently but do not boil. Use as a sauce to accompany the kebabs. Serve with green salad.

Makes 2 servings

Left: Coriander Lamb
Right: Lamb Kebabs

Lamb

Parsley Roast Leg of Lamb

1 leg of lamb (5 lb, 2 kg 240 g) trimmed of all fat

4 fl oz (110 ml) fresh lemon juice

½ oz (15 g) freshly chopped parsley

2 teaspoons dry mustard

¾ teaspoon dried rosemary

salt and pepper to taste

parsley or celery leaves for garnish

Preheat oven to 325°F, Gas Mark 3, 170°C. Place lamb on rack in roasting tin. Roast for 1 hour. Combine lemon juice, parsley, mustard and rosemary. Mix well and pour over lamb. Sprinkle with salt and pepper. Roast for 18-20 minutes to the pound for medium, 20-25 minutes per pound for medium well done. Weigh portions before serving. Garnish with parsley or celery leaves.

Makes 6 servings

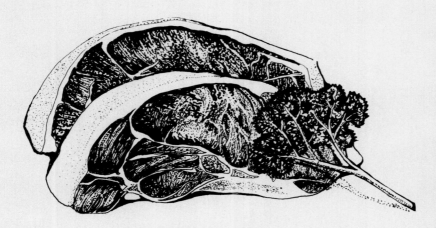

Spicy Lamb and Bean Casserole

6 oz (170 g) cooked lamb (from shoulder or leg), cubed

4 oz (110 g) onion, peeled

8 oz (230 g) cooked red kidney beans

6 oz (170 g) canned tomatoes

pinch cayenne pepper

5 fl oz (140 ml) chicken stock made with ½ cube

seasoning to taste

Preheat oven to 350°F, Gas Mark 4, 180°C. Dry-fry meat in non-stick pan, add onions and cook for a further 2 minutes. Add rest of ingredients, transfer to an ovenproof casserole, cover and bake for 45 minutes. Divide into 2 equal portions before serving.

Makes 2 servings

Savoury Yogurt Mousse

4 oz (110 g) cooked lamb, minced

1 oz (30 g) spring onions, finely chopped

2 standard eggs

5 fl oz (140 ml) natural unsweetened yogurt

salt and pepper to taste

1½ teaspoons unflavoured gelatine

cucumber and tomato for garnish

Prepare 2 individual soufflé dishes, each with a collar of greaseproof paper. Mix all ingredients except gelatine in a bowl. Dissolve the gelatine in a little hot water and add to the mixture. Divide between the prepared dishes and place in refrigerator. When set, decorate with slices of cucumber and tomato.

Makes 2 servings

Stuffed Lambs' Hearts

2 × 6 oz (170 g) lambs' hearts

salt to taste

1 teaspoon curry powder

1 teaspoon dried onion flakes

6 oz (170 g) hot cooked rice

Stuffing:

2 slices wholemeal bread
(2 oz, 60 g) made into crumbs

1 tablespoon chopped parsley

1½ oz (45 g) celery, finely chopped

grated rind of 1 lemon

salt and pepper to taste

3 tablespoons chicken stock made
with ½ cube

Preheat oven to 300°F, Gas Mark 2, 150°C. Trim the hearts and remove the sinews and fat with scissors. Snip through the centre division to make one cavity in each heart. Soak for 1 hour in salted cold water to cover. Make the stuffing by mixing all ingredients, using chicken stock to bind. Stuff the prepared hearts and close the opening with wooden cocktail sticks. Place them in a shallow ovenproof dish and add 10 fl oz (280 ml) water, curry powder and onion flakes. Cover and cook in oven for 2½ hours or until tender. Baste hearts occasionally during cooking. Drain off liquid before serving. Arrange the hot, freshly cooked rice on a serving plate. Slice cooked hearts and place on the rice. Divide into 2 equal portions.

Makes 2 servings

Braised Lambs' Tongues

2 lb (900 g) lambs' tongues

1½ pints (scant litre) water

salt and pepper to taste

bay leaf

1 clove garlic, peeled and crushed

1 pint (570 ml) chicken stock
made with 1 cube

6 oz (170 g) carrots, diced

8 oz (230 g) onion, diced

3-4 sticks celery, chopped

8 oz (230 g) peas

2 tablespoons (1 oz, 30 g)
tomato purée

6 teaspoons flour

parsley for garnish

In large saucepan combine the first 5 ingredients and bring to the boil. Cook on low heat for 1-1½ hours. Drain tongues and when cool enough, skin and slice carefully. Meanwhile combine chicken stock, carrots, onion, celery, peas and tomato purée in saucepan and cook for about 10 minutes until vegetables are tender. Mix flour with a little water, add to vegetables and cook for 2-3 minutes. Adjust seasoning. Pour vegetables into heated serving dish and lay tongue slices in overlapping layers on top. Sprinkle with parsley. Divide into 4 equal portions before serving.

Makes 4 servings

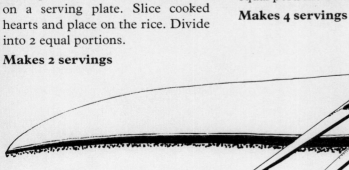

Lamb

Lamb and Sesame Korma

4 teaspoons sesame seeds
½ teaspoon salt
3 dried hot chillies
½ teaspoon cinnamon
¼ teaspoon ground cardamom
¼ teaspoon ground ginger
¼ teaspoon ground cloves
1 teaspoon garlic granules
2 teaspoons ground coriander
1 teaspoon ground cumin
5 fl oz (140 ml) water
4 oz (110 g) onion, chopped
5 fl oz (140 ml) natural unsweetened yogurt
1½ lbs (700 g) lean, cooked lamb, cut into pieces
grated rind of ½ lemon
2 teaspoons lemon juice
½ teaspoon ground turmeric
12 oz (340 g) canned tomatoes
12 oz (340 g) hot cooked rice

Brown sesame seeds in a dry pan with ½ teaspoon salt. Add chillies with a little water and crush together. Mix cinnamon, cardamom, ginger, cloves, garlic, coriander and cumin. Add to sesame seeds and chillies and mix to a paste with water. Add onion and yogurt and stir in lamb, turning well with a wooden spoon. Add lemon rind and juice, turmeric and tomatoes. Cover pan, bring to the boil and simmer over low heat for 10-15 minutes. Divide meat mixture and rice into 4 equal portions before serving.

Makes 4 servings

Right: Shasliks of Lemon Chicken Tandoori (see p. 117)

Beef

Chilli Con Carne

4 oz (110 g) onion
1 tablespoon (½ oz, 15 g) tomato purée
1 stock cube
6 oz (170 g) cooked minced beef
8 oz (230 g) cooked red beans
salt, pepper and garlic powder to taste
chilli powder to taste
2 teaspoons cornflour
6 oz (170 g) hot cooked rice

Chop the onion. Crumble stock cube into 10 fl oz (280 ml) hot water and mix in the tomato purée. Pour over the onion in a small pan and cook gently until onion is tender. Add meat, beans and seasonings. Bring to the boil and simmer for 10 minutes. Blend cornflour with a little water and add to the pan. Simmer until sauce has thickened. Place the hot rice on a serving dish and spoon the *chilli con carne* into the centre. Divide rice, meat and sauce into 2 equal portions before serving.

Makes 2 servings

Jellied Beef Mould

3 oz (80g) celery, chopped
2 oz (60 g) onion, diced
10 fl oz (280 ml) beef stock made with 1 cube
6 oz (170 g) minced cooked beef
3 oz (80 g) pickled cucumber, diced
1 teaspoon chopped parsley
2 oz (60 g) cooked peas
1 tablespoon unflavoured gelatine
salt and pepper to taste
lettuce leaves

Cook celery and onions in stock until tender but firm. Drain, reserving stock. Add celery and onions to the meat, stir in pickle and chopped parsley and mix well. Sprinkle peas on the base of an 8″ × 4″ × 3″ loaf pan. Spoon in beef mixture. Heat stock. Sprinkle in gelatine, off the heat, and stir until dissolved. Season to taste and pour over beef. Chill for 2-3 hours. Unmould and garnish with lettuce leaves.

Makes 1 serving

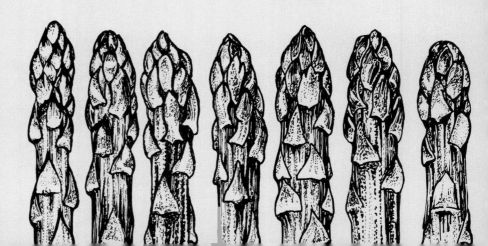

Corned Beef Stew

2 fl oz (60 ml) tomato juice

4 fl oz (110 ml) beef stock made with ½ cube

¼ teaspoon dried marjoram

1 teaspoon grated horseradish

pepper and garlic powder to taste

4 oz (110 g) canned tomatoes, drained

2 oz (60 g) canned peas, drained

2 oz (60 g) cooked onions

6 oz (170 g) corned beef, cubed

3 oz (80 g) cooked potatoes

Preheat oven to 325°F, Gas Mark 3, 170°C. In a baking dish, combine tomato juice, beef stock, marjoram, horseradish and a pinch each of pepper and garlic powder. Mix well. Add tomatoes, peas, onions and corned beef and bake, covered, for 20 minutes. Serve with potatoes.

Makes 1 serving

Beef with Asparagus

12 × 1 oz (30 g) slices beef, cooked

15 oz (430 g) canned asparagus spears, drained weight

9 oz (260 g) tomatoes, cut in quarters

celery salt

Lay slices of beef on board. Divide asparagus spears between the slices. Roll up and arrange on a large platter. Decorate with tomato quarters and sprinkle with celery salt. Divide into 3 equal portions.

Makes 3 servings

Steak Roll

1 lb (460 g) braising steak in one flat piece

2 tablespoons dried onion flakes

3 oz (80 g) mushrooms

3 oz (80 g) tomato

1 clove garlic, crushed

2 tablespoons beef stock made with ¼ cube

1 teaspoon English mustard

freshly ground black pepper to taste

salt to taste

¼ teaspoon mixed dried herbs

Preheat oven to 375°F, Gas Mark 5, 190°C. Place the steak between two sheets of polythene and beat well with a rolling pin or meat mallet until about ¼″ thick. Soak the onion flakes until softened. Wash and chop mushrooms. Skin and chop tomato. Mix the prepared vegetables with the garlic and beef stock. Spread the steak thinly with made mustard then season well with freshly ground black pepper and salt. Sprinkle with the herbs. Cover the steak with the vegetable mixture. Roll up steak like a Swiss roll and secure with skewers. Wrap roll in foil, place on a rack and bake in oven for 1¼ hours. Remove the foil from the roll for the last 20 minutes to allow it to brown. Drain off any liquid. Divide into 2 equal portions.

Makes 2 servings

Potato Crust Beef Pie

4 oz (110 g) corned beef, diced

4 oz (110 g) onion, chopped

2 oz (60 g) peas

3 oz (80 g) carrots, finely diced

3 oz (80 g) green beans, sliced

3 oz (80 g) celery, diced

salt and pepper to taste

5 fl oz (140 ml) tomato juice

Topping :

6 oz (170 g) mashed potato

6 teaspoons flour

2 oz (60 g) hard cheese, finely grated

salt and pepper

2 teaspoons margarine

Preheat oven to 350°F, Gas Mark 4, 180°C. Mix the corned beef and vegetables. Put into ovenproof casserole, sprinkle with salt and pepper to taste and pour tomato juice over. In a basin combine mashed potato, flour, grated cheese and salt and pepper. Turn mixture onto work top and pat out to cover top of pie dish. Place carefully over the meat and vegetables. Dot with margarine. Bake for 40 minutes until vegetables are tender and crust browned. Divide into 2 equal portions before serving.

Makes 2 servings

Beef

Cottage Pie

4 oz (110 g) minced cooked beef

4 fl oz (110 ml) tomato juice

4 tablespoons beef stock made with ½ cube

1½ teaspoons dried onion flakes

1½ teaspoons dried pepper flakes

1½ teaspoons dried celery flakes

salt and pepper to taste

1 teaspoon dried mixed herbs

3 oz (80 g) cooked potato

paprika

Preheat oven to 400°F, Gas Mark 6, 170°C. Place the beef in a saucepan with the tomato juice, stock, dried vegetable flakes, salt and pepper and mixed herbs. Bring to boil, stirring. Cover pan and simmer for 15 minutes. Spoon the meat mixture into an ovenproof dish, mash the cooked potato and place on top of the meat. Sprinkle with a little paprika Place in oven for 15 minutes or until top is crisp and brown.

Makes 1 serving

Left: Cottage Pie

Beef

Roast Beef Jardiniere

3 lbs (1 kg 400 g) boned sirloin beef

salt and black pepper to taste

1 clove garlic

4 fl oz (110 ml) hot water

3 sticks celery cut into 2" pieces

6 oz (170 g) spring onions cut into 2" sticks

10 fl oz (280 ml) beef stock made with 1 cube

12 oz (340 g) tomatoes

watercress for garnish

Preheat oven to 475°F, Gas Mark 9, 240°C, then reduce heat to 425°F, Gas Mark 7, 220°C.

Salt and pepper the beef. Slice garlic clove into three and insert into beef at three different places. Place beef on rack in roasting tin and pour over hot water. Cover tin with foil and roast for 50-75 minutes, or longer if preferred well done. Meanwhile poach celery and spring onions in stock. Add sliced tomatoes. When meat has cooked, turn oven off and leave meat inside for a further 10 minutes. Drain vegetables and arrange round the meat on a heated dish. Garnish with watercress. Divide meat and vegetables into 6 equal portions before serving.

Makes 6 servings

Ox Heart in Savoury Sauce

12 oz (340 g) ox heart

15 fl oz (430 ml) water

salt and pepper to taste

1 teaspoon pickling spice

1 clove garlic

1 tablespoon dried onion flakes

1 bay leaf

1 tablespoon vinegar

4 oz (110 g) carrots

2 oz (60 g) parsnips

2 oz (60 g) swede

3 oz (80 g) celery

6 oz (170 g) cooked potatoes

Soak ox heart in salted water for 1 hour. Drain and transfer to a saucepan. Add water, salt and pepper, herbs, spices and vinegar. Bring to the boil and simmer for 2½-3 hours. Peel and dice carrots, parsnips and swede. Cut celery into fine dice. Cook vegetables in boiling salted water to cover for 5-10 minutes or until soft. Drain and reserve. When the heart is cooked, drain cooking liquid into a shallow dish and cool in the freezer compartment of the refrigerator. Meanwhile, cut the heart into fine strips and reserve, covered, in a cool place. When the cooking liquid is quite cold, remove all visible fat. Measure 12 fl oz (340 ml) liquid into blender goblet, add cooked vegetables and blend until smooth. Transfer to a saucepan, add strips of heart, bring to the boil and simmer for 15 minutes. Serve with potatoes. Divide into 2 equal portions.

Makes 2 servings

Corned Beefburgers

4 oz (110 g) corned beef

2 slices bread (2 oz, 60 g) made into crumbs

2 standard eggs

1 teaspoon dry mustard

salt and pepper to taste

1 teaspoon dried basil

2 teaspoons flour

Mash corned beef with a fork. Add breadcrumbs and mix well. Beat eggs with mustard, salt and pepper and basil. Add to bread and meat mixture and beat well. Sprinkle flour on a board or worktop and shape the mixture into 4 flat cakes. Cook under a hot grill for 3 minutes each side or until crisp and golden. Serve with mixed salad. Divide into 2 equal portions.

Makes 2 servings

Farmer's Lunch

3 oz (80 g) small potatoes

1 oz (30 g) onion

2 oz (60 g) corned beef

1 standard egg

salt to taste

1 teaspoon chopped chives

1 pickled cucumber

Peel potatoes and slice thinly. Chop onion finely and poach potatoes and onions in a little water in a non-stick pan until just soft. Drain off water. Cut corned beef into cubes and add to pan. Beat egg and pour over the meat mixture. Continue cooking over low heat until egg is set, then sprinkle with salt and chives. Serve with sliced, pickled cucumber.

Makes 1 serving

Barbecued Beefburgers

1 lb (460 g) lean, minced beef

2 teaspoons dried onion flakes

¼ teaspoon garlic flakes

salt and black pepper to taste

Beat all ingredients well together in mixing bowl. Divide evenly into 4 flat cakes and cook on barbecue or grill on a rack, for approximately 5 minutes on each side. Serve with Barbecue Sauce.* Divide into 2 equal portions.

Makes 2 servings
*See page 106 for sauce recipe.

Old English Stuffed Marrow

10 fl oz (280 ml) beef stock made with 1 cube

2 teaspoons dried onion flakes

8 oz (230 g) mushrooms, sliced

6 oz (170 g) carrots, sliced

1 teaspoon dried basil

½ teaspoon black pepper

1 vegetable marrow

4 tablespoons (2 oz, 60 g) tomato purée

1½ lbs (700 g) cooked minced beef

6 oz (170 g) tomatoes, halved

Preheat oven to 425°F, Gas Mark 7, 220°C. Place stock, onion flakes, mushrooms, carrots, basil and pepper in saucepan. Bring to boil and cook until vegetables are tender. Cut marrow in half lengthwise, peel and remove pith and pips. When vegetables are cooked, add tomato purée and minced beef. Mix well and fill each half of marrow with mixture. Press halves together and wrap in foil. Place on baking sheet and bake for 60-75 minutes. Grill tomato halves and arrange round cooked, stuffed marrow. Divide into 4 equal portions. Serve at once.

Makes 4 servings

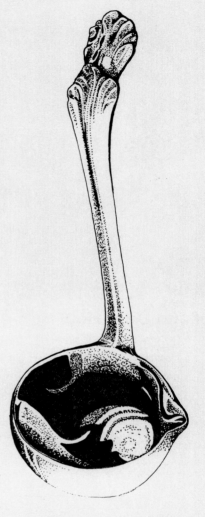

Beef and Bean Hot Pot

4 oz (110 g) onion
3 oz (80 g) carrots
½ beef stock cube
6 fl oz (170 ml) water
1 teaspoon dried marjoram or basil
2 teaspoons chopped parsley
4 oz (110 g) cooked minced beef
6 oz (170 g) canned butter beans, drained weight
3 oz (80 g) canned tomatoes, drained weight
salt and pepper to taste
6 oz (170 g) cooked potato, sliced

Preheat oven to 400°F, Gas Mark 6, 200°C. Finely chop onion and carrots and place in pan with stock cube, water and herbs. Bring to boil and simmer until vegetables are tender. Place minced beef and beans in ovenproof casserole, stir in cooked vegetables and tomatoes. Season to taste, cover with sliced potatoes and bake for 20 minutes, or until potato is crispy and brown. Divide into 2 equal portions before serving.

Makes 2 servings

Spicy Mince with Spaghetti

1 teaspoon sage
1 clove garlic, crushed
artificial sweetener to taste
½ teaspoon curry powder
1 teaspoon Worcester sauce
4 tablespoons (2 oz, 60 g) tomato purée
10 fl oz (280 ml) water
1 beef stock cube
4 oz (110 g) onion
6 oz (170 g) cooked minced beef
3 oz (80 g) hot cooked spaghetti
1 teaspoon vegetable oil

Place first 9 ingredients in a saucepan and bring to the boil. Simmer until sauce is thick, add mince, mix well and simmer for a further 10 minutes. Toss spaghetti in oil, pile onto serving dish and serve with sauce.

Makes 1 serving

Above: Spicy Mince with Spaghetti
Right: Beef and Bean Hot Pot

Beef

Stuffed Cabbage

4-6 large cabbage leaves
(4-6 oz, 110-170 g)

4 oz (110 g) cooked minced beef

3 oz (80 g) cooked rice

2 teaspoons onion flakes

1 teaspoon Worcester sauce

1 tablespoon chopped parsley

10 fl oz (280 ml) stock made with
1 beef cube

salt and pepper to taste

Preheat oven to 350°F, Gas Mark 4, 180°C. Blanch cabbage leaves in boiling, salted water for 2 minutes. Lift out and drain on kitchen paper. Mix beef with rice, onion flakes, Worcester sauce and parsley. Divide equally between cabbage leaves, roll up and secure with wooden cocktail sticks. Place in ovenproof casserole, pour stock over the rolls, season to taste, cover and cook in oven for 1-1½ hours.

Makes 1 serving

Kidneys in Watercress Sauce

2 bunches watercress

10 fl oz (280 ml) chicken stock made
with ½ cube

1½ lbs (700 g) ox kidney, trimmed*

8 oz (230 g) onions

salt to taste

6 oz (170 g) green pepper

6 oz (170 g) mushrooms

2 tablespoons flour

Preheat oven to 350°F, Gas Mark 4 180°C. Wash watercress and discard any discoloured leaves. Chop roughly and put in saucepan, add stock, bring to boil and simmer for 10 minutes. Transfer to blender and blend well. Set aside. Dice kidney. Sprinkle non-stick pan with light covering of salt, carefully add kidney and cook over medium heat, shaking the pan to prevent sticking. Peel and dice onion and add to kidney. Continue cooking, shaking pan and stirring the contents. De-seed pepper and cut into strips. Wash and slice mushrooms. Add to the pan and cook for a further 3-4 minutes. Transfer contents to a 4-pint oven-proof casserole. Mix flour with a little water, add to stock and watercress mixture and stir well. Pour over contents of casserole, cover and bake for 1-1½ hours or until kidney is tender. Divide into 4 equal portions.

* Cut ox kidney in half lengthwise with scissors and snip out the stringy core.

Makes 4 servings

Meatballs in Tomato Sauce

4 slices bread (4 oz, 110 g)
4 tablespoons skim milk
4 oz (110 g) onion
1½ lbs (700 g) minced beef
1 teaspoon ground allspice
1 teaspoon curry powder
2 teaspoons Worcester sauce
salt and pepper to taste
12 oz (340 g) hot cooked rice

Sauce:

1 lb (460 g) ripe tomatoes
1 tablespoon lemon juice
1 beef stock cube
artificial sweetener to taste

Preheat oven to 350°F, Gas Mark 4, 180°C. Place bread slices in a shallow dish with milk. Mix finely chopped onion with the minced beef, add rest of seasonings and mix well. Squeeze the bread well and fork into the meat. Knead the mixture together, divide into 12 equal pieces and roll into balls. Place on rack in ovenproof dish and bake for 40-45 minutes. Meanwhile, pour boiling water over tomatoes, leave for 1 minute, drain well and skin. Place tomatoes in blender with lemon juice, stock cube and sweetener, and blend for 2 minutes. Turn into a saucepan and bring to boil. Simmer for 3 minutes. Make a bed of rice on a heated dish, remove meatballs from rack and arrange on top. Spoon sauce over meatballs. Divide meatballs, sauce and rice into 4 equal portions and serve at once.

Makes 4 servings

Spaghetti Bolognaise

12 fl oz (340 ml) tomato juice
¼ teaspoon dried oregano
1 bay leaf
¼ teaspoon garlic salt
artificial sweetener to taste
8 oz (230 g) cooked minced beef
6 oz (170 g) hot cooked spaghetti
parsley for garnish

Place the tomato juice in a saucepan with the oregano, bay leaf, garlic salt, artificial sweetener and minced meat. Bring to the boil, cover and simmer for 25 minutes. Discard the bay leaf. Arrange the hot, freshly cooked spaghetti on a serving dish. Pour the sauce over the spaghetti. Divide into 2 equal portions and serve garnished with parsley.

Makes 2 servings

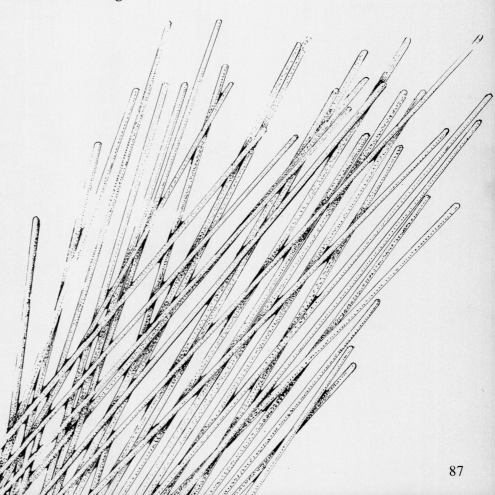

Beef

Roman Holiday Sausages

4 oz (110 g) diced onion

12 oz (340 g) canned tomatoes

1 clove garlic, crushed

oregano to taste

12 oz (340 g) beef sausages

6 oz (170 g) hot cooked rice

In non-stick pan, cook onions over gentle heat until transparent. Add all other ingredients except sausages and rice. Bring to boil and simmer for 15-20 mintes until reduced to a thick sauce. Meanwhile, grill sausages until cooked through and brown on all sides. To serve, place sausages on bed of rice and pour tomato sauce over. Divide sausages, rice and sauce into 2 equal portions before serving.

Makes 2 servings

Right: Roman Holiday Sausages

Pork

Super Stuffed Pork Chops

4 × 5 oz (140 g) pork chops, trimmed of all fat

salt, pepper and garlic powder to taste

1 medium apple, peeled, cored and diced

8 fl oz (230 ml) chicken stock made with 1 cube

6 oz (170 g) cooked rice

pinch cinnamon

pinch chicken seasoning

1 teaspoon dried onion flakes

Preheat oven to 375°F, Gas Mark 5, 190°C. Preheat grill. Season chops with salt, pepper and garlic powder. Place on a rack and grill about 4″ from source of heat until chops are brown on both sides. Remove from grill pan. Combine apple and stock in a saucepan and cook until apple is tender. Drain and mix thoroughly with the rice, cinnamon, chicken seasoning, onion flakes, salt and pepper. Divide stuffing mixture into 4 even portions and place one portion on each chop. Arrange chops in ovenproof dish and bake for 20 minutes or until stuffing is brown and chops thoroughly cooked.

Makes 2 servings

Party Frankfurters

1 oz (30 g) onion, finely chopped

3 oz (80 g) cooked potato, diced

1 tablespoon mayonnaise

1 teaspoon curry powder

4 oz (110 g) frankfurters, sliced

3 oz pickled cucumber, sliced

2 oz (60 g) silver skin pickled onions

Mix chopped onion and potato together. Combine mayonnaise and curry powder and pour over potato. Arrange on a dinner plate with the frankfurters, cucumber slices and silver skin onions.

Makes 1 serving

Roast Loin of Pork

2 lbs (900 g) boned loin pork, rolled

3 cloves garlic, peeled and cut in slivers

sprigs of parsley

salt and freshly ground pepper to taste

1 teaspoon dried rosemary

Preheat oven to 325°F, Gas Mark 3, 170°C. With a sharp knife, make several cuts across the top of the roast, about 1½″ in depth, and insert garlic slivers and parsley into each cut. Season with salt and pepper and rosemary. Roast on a rack in the oven for approximately 1½-2 hours. Weigh portions.

Makes 4 servings

Sweet and Sour Pork Fillet with Beansprouts

1½ lb (700 g) pork fillet

1 × 15 oz (430 g) can beansprouts, drained

2 tablespoons soy sauce

black pepper to taste

For sauce:

1½ tablespoons wine vinegar

1½ tablespoons lemon juice

4 oz (110 g) tomato purée

artificial sweetener to taste

2 teaspoons paprika

10 fl oz (280 ml) water

3 oz (80 g) carrots, cut into fine strips

3 oz (80 g) green pepper, finely sliced

2 teaspoons arrowroot

Cut the pork fillet into cubes and grill on rack on a sheet of foil pierced at intervals to allow the juices to drip away. Turn the pork frequently until thoroughly cooked. Place on serving dish and keep hot. Mix soy sauce, beansprouts and black pepper and heat through in a small pan, stirring constantly. Turn into a serving dish, cover and keep hot. To make the sauce, combine all ingredients except arrowroot in a small pan. Bring to the boil and simmer for 20 minutes. Mix the arrowroot with a little water, add to the sauce and cook for 2 minutes. Pour over the pork and serve with the beansprouts. Divide into 4 equal portions.

Makes 4 servings

Pork and Apple Bake

4 × 10 oz (280 g) pork loin chops

8 oz (230 g) onions, sliced

3 oz (80 g) mushrooms, chopped

10 fl oz (280 ml) chicken stock, made with 1 cube

12 oz (340 g) carrots, sliced

1 medium cooking apple, peeled, cored and sliced

salt, black pepper and mixed herbs to taste

10 fl oz (280 ml) natural, unsweetened yogurt

12 oz (340 g) potatoes, cut into thin slices

Preheat grill and preheat oven to 300°F, Gas Mark 2, 150°C. Grill chops on a rack 10 minutes each side. Transfer to a casserole dish. Cook onions and mushrooms lightly in a little of the chicken stock. Add to casserole with remaining stock, carrots and apple. Add salt, pepper and herbs to taste. Cover with yogurt and top with potatoes. Cover dish and bake for 2 hours. Turn oven heat up to 450°F, Gas Mark 8, 230°C and bake casserole uncovered for a further 20 minutes. Serve with broccoli or cabbage. Divide into 4 equal portions.

Makes 4 servings

Frankfurter Rice Salad

6 oz (170 g) cooked rice

8 oz (230 g) cooked peas

8 oz (230 g) frankfurters, sliced diagonally

3 oz (80 g) red pepper, sliced

3 oz (80 g) tomato, sliced

2 sticks celery, chopped

Dressing:

2 teaspoons vegetable oil

6 teaspoons lemon juice

large pinch dry mustard

salt and pepper to taste

dash hot sauce or Worcester sauce

Place all ingredients for dressing in a screw top jar and shake thoroughly. Pour dressing over rice, peas and frankfurters, toss well together, cover and chill. To serve, divide evenly between 2 plates and decorate with red pepper, tomato and celery. Serve with green salad.

Makes 2 servings

Orange Baked Pork Chops

2 × 5 oz (140 g) pork chops, trimmed

salt and pepper to taste

2 oz (60 g) onion, sliced

2 fl oz (60 ml) tomato juice

artificial sweetener to taste

1 teaspoon grated lemon rind

1 medium orange, sliced in rings

pinch dried marjoram

parsley for garnish

Preheat oven to 400°F, Gas Mark 6, 200°C, and preheat grill. Season chops and grill on rack 4″ from source of heat for 4-5 minutes on each side until brown. Turn off grill and place chops in small baking dish. Add onions, tomato juice, artificial sweetener and lemon rind. Arrange orange rings on top, sprinkle with marjoram and bake, covered, for 20 minutes or until meat is cooked through and onions are tender. Serve piping hot garnished with parsley.

Makes 1 serving

Ham Omelette

4 oz (110 g) canned pineapple chunks, no sugar added

1 standard egg

1 tablespoon water

salt and pepper to taste

1½ oz (45 g) cooked ham

2 teaspoons chopped chives

3 oz (80 g) tomatoes for garnish

watercress for garnish

Drain pineapple chunks. Whisk egg with water, salt and pepper. Pour into heated non-stick pan. When egg mixture begins to set, spoon in ham, pineapple and chives and finish cooking. Fold omelette over, slide onto a heated plate and garnish with tomato and watercress.

Makes 1 serving

Above: Ham Omelette
Right: Orange Baked Pork Chops

Pork

Quick Pork Supper

1 teaspoon dried onion flakes

1½ oz (45 g) red pepper, diced

3 oz (80 g) cooked potato, diced

salt to taste

pinch pepper and paprika

½ beef stock cube

6 fl oz (170 ml) water

6 oz (170 g) pork, cubed

Combine onion, red pepper, potato, salt and pepper, paprika, stock cube and water in a non-stick pan. Heat slowly and cook over low heat, stirring occasionally, for 5 minutes or until red pepper is soft. Add pork and cook for a further 15 minutes or until pork is completely cooked. Serve with green vegetables.

Makes 1 serving

Pork Chops with Fruit Stuffing

2 × 10 oz (280 g) pork chops, well trimmed

salt and pepper to taste

garlic powder to taste

1 medium apple, peeled, cored and diced

4 medium prunes, stoned and chopped

8 fl oz (230 ml) chicken stock made with 1 cube

6 oz (170 g) cooked rice

pinch cinnamon

pinch chicken seasoning

1 teaspoon dried onion flakes

Preheat oven to 375°F, Gas Mark 5, 190°C. Season the chops with salt, pepper and garlic powder. Place on a rack and grill about 4″ from source of heat until brown on both sides. Remove from grill. Combine the apple, chopped prunes and stock in a saucepan and cook until tender. Drain and place in a mixing bowl. Add the rice, cinnamon, chicken seasoning, onion flakes, salt and pepper and mix thoroughly. Place half the stuffing on each chop and bake in oven for about 15-20 minutes.

Makes 2 servings

Roast Pork with Spiced Apricots

2½ lb (1 kg 200 g) loin of pork
1 teaspoon sage
1 teaspoon thyme
½ teaspoon garlic salt
36 cloves
12 medium apricots
artificial sweetener to taste
bunch watercress

Preheat oven to 325°F, Gas Mark 3, 170°C. Sprinkle the joint with sage, thyme and garlic salt. Place on rack in oven and cook for 1½-2 hours. Press 3 cloves into each apricot and arrange in a casserole. Add water to come halfway up the apricots and artificial sweetener to taste. Cover the casserole with a lid and cook in the oven until fruit is soft but not broken. Place cooked pork on a serving dish and garnish with spiced apricots and watercress. Serve with peas, carrots and jacket potatoes. Divide into 4 equal portions.

Makes 4 servings

Ham and Cabbage

3 teaspoons margarine
1 tablespoon cider vinegar
artificial sweetener to taste
salt and pepper to taste
6 oz (170 g) cooked shredded cabbage
4 oz (110 g) cooked ham, diced

Preheat oven to 400°F, Gas Mark 6, 200°C. Melt margarine in a basin over hot water and mix in the vinegar, sweetener, salt and pepper. Place cabbage and ham in an ovenproof dish and stir together with a fork. Pour margarine mixture over, cover dish and bake for 15 minutes.

Makes 1 serving

Hot Dog Potato Salad

4 oz (110 g) frankfurters
3 oz (80 g) potatoes, cooked
2 oz (60 g) spring onions, chopped
½ teaspoon celery seed
1 tablespoon wine vinegar
1 tablespoon vegetable oil
1 teaspoon prepared mustard

Grill frankfurters, turning occasionally until browned on all sides and cooked through. Set aside to cool. Dice potatoes, place in basin, add chopped spring onions and sprinkle with celery seed. Slice cooled frankfurters and add to potatoes. Mix wine vinegar, oil and mustard together thoroughly. Pour over salad mixture and toss so that ingredients are well coated. Chill lightly before serving.

Makes 1 serving

Sweet and Sour Ham

2 slices canned pineapple, no sugar added, with 2 tablespoons juice

4 × 1 oz (30 g) slices ham

4 fl oz (110 ml) tomato juice

2 teaspoons arrowroot

Preheat oven to 375°F, Gas Mark 5, 190°C. Cut pineapple into small pieces, lay ham flat on board, divide pineapple pieces evenly between ham slices. Roll up and secure with wooden cocktail sticks. Place side by side in an ovenproof dish. Bring tomato juice to the boil in a small saucepan. Mix arrowroot with pineapple juice, add to boiling tomato juice and cook, stirring, for 2 minutes. Pour over ham rolls and place in oven for 20 minutes or until thoroughly hot. Serve at once with salad.

Makes 1 serving

Left: Sweet and Sour Ham

Liver

Liver Special

1 lb (460 g) calf's liver, thinly sliced

3 tablespoons lemon juice

4 oz (110 g) onion, chopped

2 cloves garlic, crushed

12 oz (340 g) canned tomatoes

1 teaspoon dried sage

1 teaspoon dried basil

1 chicken stock cube

10 fl oz (280 ml) water

black pepper to taste

4 teaspoons cornflour, mixed with a little water

5 fl oz (140 ml) natural unsweetened yogurt

Place liver in a dish with lemon juice for 30 minutes, turning occasionally. Place rest of ingredients except cornflour in saucepan and add drained liver. Cook for 20 minutes. Remove liver and keep hot. Add cornflour to sauce, simmer until thickened and pour over liver. Top with yogurt. Divide into 2 equal portions.

Makes 2 servings

Liver Supreme

6 oz (170 g) chicken liver

2 teaspoons dried onion flakes

1 teaspoon dried basil

4 fl oz (110 ml) water

½ chicken stock cube

pinch pepper

1 slice bread (1 oz, 30 g) made into crumbs

2 teaspoons Worcester sauce

1 tablespoon mayonnaise

2 teaspoons unflavoured gelatine

radish slices and lettuce for garnish

Slice liver and place in small saucepan with the onion flakes, basil, water, crumbled stock cube and pepper. Bring to boil, cover pan and cook for 10 minutes or until liver is cooked through. Drain liver and reserve liquid. Roughly chop liver, place in blender goblet, add breadcrumbs, Worcester sauce, mayonnaise and half the cooking liquid. Reheat remaining cooking liquid. Sprinkle in the gelatine, off the heat, and stir until dissolved. Add mixture to contents of blender goblet and blend until smooth. Pour into a wetted 1-pint jelly mould, place in refrigerator until well chilled and firm. Unmould onto lettuce leaves and decorate with radish slices.

Makes 1 serving

Mock Goose

6 oz (170 g) liver

1½ teaspoons flour, seasoned with salt and pepper

1 oz (30 g) onion

1 medium cooking apple, peeled

3 oz (80 g) peeled potato

½ teaspoon dried sage

5 fl oz (140 ml) water or stock made with ½ cube

seasoning salt and pepper to taste

parsley for garnish

Preheat oven to 350°F, Gas Mark 4, 180°C. Dip liver in seasoned flour and place in baking dish. Slice onion, apple and potato. Spread onion over the liver, followed by a layer of apple. Sprinkle with sage. Place a layer of potato over sage and apple. Add the water or stock with seasoning salt and pepper. Cover baking dish with lid or foil and bake for 40 minutes. Towards end of cooking, uncover and allow potatoes to brown. Garnish with parsley.

Makes 1 serving

Liver with Barbecue Sauce

3 tablespoons beef stock, made with ¼ cube

1 lb (460 g) ox liver

4 oz (110 g) onion, cut in wedges

1 clove garlic, chopped

1 recipe Barbecue Sauce*

4 fl oz (110 ml) water

1½ teaspocns grated horseradish

½ teaspoon prepared mustard

Bring stock to the boil in a non-stick pan. Add liver and quickly brown on all sides turning frequently. Remove liver from pan, cut into strips, add onions and garlic to pan and cook over low heat for 5 minutes or until onions are tender but still crisp. Stir in Barbecue Sauce, water, horseradish and mustard. Cook 2 minutes. Add liver strips and simmer for 5-10 minutes or until liver is cooked through. Divide into 2 equal portions.

Makes 2 servings

*See page 106 for sauce recipe.

Chicken Liver Espagnol

6 oz (170 g) tomatoes

3 oz (80 g) red pepper

6 oz (170 g) mushrooms

12 fl oz (340 ml) tomato juice

½ stock cube

1 tablespoon dried onion flakes

1 clove garlic (optional)

pinch mace

1 lb (460 g) chicken livers

salt and pepper to taste

Peel and chop tomatoes, chop pepper and mushrooms, place in large pan, add tomato juice, stock cube, onion flakes, garlic and mace. Simmer until vegetables soften (about 5 minutes). Add chicken livers and cook over medium heat, turning livers constantly, until cooked but not hard (about 5-10 minutes according to taste). Livers should still be slightly pink inside and tender. Adjust seasoning and serve. Divide into 2 equal portions.

Makes 2 servings

Liver

Liver with Mixed Vegetables

4 fl oz (110 ml) tomato juice

1 chicken stock cube

8 oz (230 g) liver, sliced

2 oz (60 g) mushrooms, chopped

1 stick celery, chopped

½ teaspoon mixed dried herbs

2 oz (60 g) peas

1 oz (30 g) onion, chopped

3 oz (80 g) carrots, chopped

Heat tomato juice in saucepan. Crumble in stock cube. Add liver, mushrooms, celery and herbs. Cover and simmer for 10 minutes, stirring occasionally. Cook peas, onion and carrots separately. Drain and add to liver before serving.

Makes 1 serving

Left: Liver with Mixed Vegetables

Liver

Sweet Sour Liver

6 oz (170 g) liver

2 oz (60 g) onion

1 fl oz (30 ml) buttermilk

salt and pepper to taste

wine vinegar and artificial sweetener to taste

3 oz (80 g) boiled new potatoes

6 oz (170 g) cucumber

parsley

Cut liver into thin strips, chop onion and place both in non-stick pan. Dry-fry rapidly on high heat, turning constantly. When brown, add a little water and cook until tender. Add buttermilk, salt, pepper, vinegar and sweetener to taste. Serve with new potatoes and cucumber slices and garnish with parsley.

Makes 1 serving

Faggots with Gravy

8 oz (230 g) lamb's liver

1 slice bread (1 oz, 30 g) made into crumbs

1 teaspoon onion flakes

thyme, salt and pepper to taste

Gravy:

½ beef stock cube

5 fl oz (140 ml) water

pinch mixed herbs

2 teaspoons cornflour

Preheat oven to 375°F, Gas Mark 5, 190°C. Blanch liver in boiling water for 2 minutes, drain and cool. Mince liver and mix with breadcrumbs, onion flakes and seasoning. Make into mounds on flat ovenproof dish or baking tin and bake for 20 minutes until firm. Place stock cube, water and herbs in saucepan. Bring to boil, mix cornflour with 1 tablespoon water, add to stock and cook, stirring, for 2 minutes. Serve with the faggots.

Makes 1 serving

Liver with Rice

1 lb (460 g) liver, diced

2 teaspoons onion flakes

pinch garlic powder

1 pint (570 ml) chicken stock made with 1 cube

2 tablespoons (1 oz, 30 g) tomato purée

6 oz (170 g) cooked rice

Place all ingredients except rice in a 2-pint saucepan and bring to the boil. Simmer gently until liver is cooked, 10-15 minutes. Add rice for last 5 minutes of cooking time. Divide into 2 equal portions.

Makes 2 servings

Liver with Onion and Tomato Sauce

8 oz (230 g) onions

3 oz (80 g) green or red pepper (optional)

12 oz (340 g) pig's liver

10 fl oz (280 ml) stock made with 1 cube, any flavour

6 oz (170 g) canned tomatoes, chopped

salt and pepper to taste

sprigs of parsley for garnish

Peel and chop onions and pepper. Dry-fry gently in non-stick pan until lightly browned. Add liver and seal. Mix stock with tomatoes and pour over liver and onions. Cover and simmer for approximately 15 minutes, stirring occasionally. Season to taste. Turn heat up and cook for a further 10-15 minutes, stirring frequently until stock is reduced to a thick gravy. Garnish with parsley, divide into 2 equal portions and serve with vegetable of your choice.

Makes 2 servings.

Cabbage Rolls

12 oz (340 g) liver, in slices

1 tablespoon dried onion flakes

pepper to taste

1 beef stock cube, crumbled

10 fl. oz (280 ml) water

1 teaspoon mixed dried herbs

4 medium cabbage leaves

2 slices bread (2 oz, 60 g) made into crumbs

Preheat oven to 425°F, Gas Mark 7, 220°C. Place liver, onion flakes, pepper, crumbled stock cube, water and herbs in saucepan, bring to the boil and simmer for 5 minutes. Blanch cabbage leaves for 2 minutes in boiling, salted water, lift out and leave to drain on kitchen towel on a flat board. Carefully remove liver slices from cooking liquid, mince or chop finely and put into a basin. Strain liquid and reserve. Add onion and herbs to liver. Add bread-crumbs and a little cooking liquid and beat together thoroughly. Divide into four sausage shapes, place each in centre of cabbage leaf, fold up like a parcel and place in ovenproof casserole. Pour over remainder of cooking liquid, cover with foil or lid and bake in oven for 30 minutes. Divide into 2 equal portions.

Makes 2 servings

Liver and Apple Casserole

1 teaspoon dried onion flakes

1 medium cooking apple

8 oz (230 g) lamb's liver

salt and pepper to taste

8 fl oz (230 ml) tomato juice

3 oz (80 g) tomato

3 oz (80 g) hot cooked rice

Preheat oven to 350°F, Gas Mark 4, 180°C. Sprinkle the onion flakes over the base of an ovenproof casserole. Slice the apple and arrange half the slices on top of the onion. Slice the liver. Season and place it on the apple. Top with the remaining apple slices and pour in the tomato juice. Cover and bake for 30 minutes. Slice the tomato and arrange on top of the apple. Return the casserole to the oven and cook, uncovered, for a further 5 minutes. Serve with the hot rice.

Makes 1 serving

● When buying liver, make sure that it is fresh and avoid any which has a bluish tint.

● For a piquant flavour sprinkle a little finely chopped fresh sage leaves over liver while dry-frying.

● When dry-frying liver, remember that overcooking will toughen it. It should be taken up while still pink in the centre.

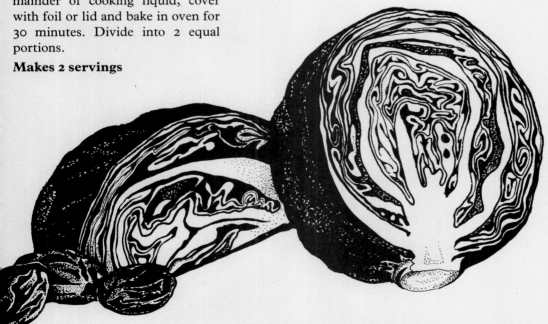

Liver

Liver Kebabs

1 lb (460 g) liver

1 teaspoon salt

pepper to taste

6 oz (170 g) small tomatoes

3 oz (80 g) mushroom caps

3 oz (80 g) green pepper, cut in squares

2 oz (60 g) shallots

1½ tablespoons lemon juice

2 tablespoons chicken stock made with ¼ cube

Cut liver into cubes, sprinkle with seasonings. Thread liver and vegetables alternately on two skewers. Sprinkle with lemon juice and stock and grill until cooked through.

Makes 2 servings

Right: Stuffed Liver

104

Liver

Stuffed Liver

2 slices bread (2 oz, 60 g) made into crumbs

2 teaspoons onion flakes

1 tablespoon chopped parsley

rind of 1 lemon, grated

6 teaspoons margarine

juice of 1 lemon

1 lb (460 g) liver, cut into thin slices

10 fl oz (280 ml) stock made with 1 beef cube

3 teaspoons arrowroot

Preheat oven to 425°F, Gas Mark 7, 220°C. Combine breadcrumbs, onion flakes, parsley and lemon rind. Melt margarine in cup over hot water, add lemon juice, pour into breadcrub mixture and mix well. Leave to cool. Lay slices of liver flat, divide stuffing evenly between each piece, roll up and secure with a toothpick. If using thick slices of liver, slit down centre to make pocket and fill with stuffing. Place in ovenproof casserole, pour stock over liver and bake for 25 minutes. Mix arrowroot with 1 tablespoon of water and stir carefully into the casserole. Replace in oven for 5 minutes to allow sauce to thicken. Divide into 2 equal portions.

Makes 2 servings

Sauces for Meat

Leek and Tomato Sauce

4 oz (110 g) leeks

3 oz (80 g) tomato

salt and pepper to taste

Chop leeks finely, place in small saucepan, add water to cover and salt to taste. Bring to boil and cook for 8-10 minutes until soft. Drain. Skin and chop tomato, add to leeks, add pepper to taste. Mix thoroughly and serve cold with meat or poultry.

Makes 1 serving

Onion Sauce

6 oz (170 g) onion, chopped

6 teaspoons margarine

6 teaspoons flour

10 fl oz (280 ml) skim milk

salt and pepper to taste

Cook onion in water until soft. Drain and reserve cooking water. Melt margarine in top of double boiler over boiling water. Stir in flour, milk and seasoning. Cook over low heat until thickened. Stir in onion and add some of the cooking water if sauce is too thick. Cook for a further 2 minutes. Divide evenly. Serve with roast lamb.

Makes 6 servings

Mustard Fruit Sauce

8 fl oz (230 ml) tomato juice

8 fl oz (230 ml) orange juice

1 teaspoon white vinegar

artificial sweetener to taste

1 teaspoon dry mustard

pinch cinnamon

dash brown food colouring

Combine all ingredients except cinnamon and food colouring. Simmer over medium heat until mixture is reduced by half. Add cinnamon and colouring as desired. Divide sauce into 4 equal portions. Good with ham or pork.

Makes 4 servings

Mint Sauce

2 tablespoons chopped mint

2 tablespoons lemon juice

2 tablespoons cider vinegar

artificial sweetener to taste

Combine all ingredients in a small bowl. Leave to stand for one hour.

Makes 4 servings

Barbecue Sauce

16 fl oz (460 ml) tomato juice

2 teaspoons vinegar

1 teaspoon Worcester sauce

2 teaspoons lemon juice

4 teaspoons tomato ketchup

artificial sweetener to taste

¼ teaspoon dry mustard

pinch pepper and salt

Combine all ingredients in a saucepan. Simmer for 20 minutes or until mixture is reduced to half original volume. Good with beefburgers. Divide evenly.

Makes 4 servings

All Purpose Sauce

2 tablespoons dried onion flakes

1 teaspoon mixed dried herbs

1 teaspoon salt

¼ teaspoon black pepper

artificial sweetener to taste

12 oz (340 g) canned tomatoes

2 teaspoons cornflour mixed with a little water

Bring all ingredients to boil in a saucepan and cook until onion is soft. This is a basic sauce to which additional flavourings such as curry powder may be added. Divide evenly.

Makes 2 servings

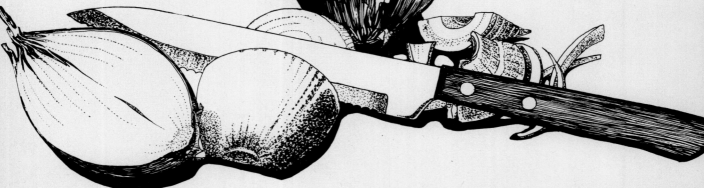

Flamenco Sauce

1-3 cloves garlic, crushed

1 tablespoon dried onion flakes

4 fl oz (110 ml) tomato juice

1 stick celery

3 oz (80 g) red pepper

3 oz (80 g) mushrooms

salt and freshly ground black pepper to taste

Bring the garlic, onion flakes and tomato juice to the boil in a saucepan and simmer for 10 minutes. Chop celery. Remove membranes and seeds from pepper and slice thinly. Wash mushrooms and cut into quarters. Add prepared vegetables to saucepan with salt and pepper. Cook for a further 10 minutes or until vegetables are cooked but still crisp. Serve with grilled steak.

Makes 1 serving

Curry Sauce

6 oz (170 g) green pepper, de-seeded

4 sticks celery

2 tablespoons dried onion flakes

12 fl oz (340 g) tomato juice

2 chicken stock cubes

salt and pepper to taste

6 oz (170 g) canned red peppers

1-2 teaspoons curry powder

artificial sweetener to taste

Slice green pepper and celery. Place in a saucepan with the onion flakes, tomato juice, stock cubes, salt and pepper, and simmer gently until tender. Chop red peppers and add to the pan with curry powder and sweetener. Stir well. Leave to cool and press the mixture through a sieve or blend at high speed in blender. Store in screw-top jars in refrigerator. Divide into 4 equal portions.

Makes 4 servings

Celery Sauce

1 head celery, thinly sliced

1½ pints (scant litre) beef stock made with 3 cubes

Cook celery in the stock until soft – about 15 minutes. Turn into blender goblet and blend until smooth. Return to saucepan and simmer until thickened. Divide evenly. Very good with roast lamb.

Makes 6 servings

Mango Cooler

½ small mango

5 fl oz (140 ml) natural unsweetened yogurt

salt to taste

½ teaspoon margarine

½ teaspoon mustard seed, crushed

1 green chilli, very finely chopped

pinch ground coriander

Peel and dice mango. Add to yogurt with salt. Put margarine into small bowl over pan of hot water, add crushed mustard seed and chopped chilli and stir well. Stir into yogurt mixture. Chill lightly until required. Sprinkle with coriander before serving.

Makes 1 serving

Horseradish Sauce

2 teaspoons grated horseradish

1 tablespoon cider vinegar

3 tablespoons lemon juice

5 fl oz (140 ml) water

artificial sweetener to taste

1 teaspoon salt

1 teaspoon paprika

6 oz (170 g) nonfat dry milk

Place all ingredients in blender and mix at high speed for 30 seconds or until sauce is well blended. Divide evenly.

Makes 6 servings

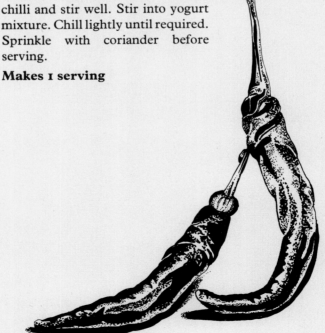

Poultry, Veal and Game

Poultry, Veal and Game

Chicken Curry

½ teaspoon curry powder

½ teaspoon garam masala

½ teaspoon chilli powder, or to taste

2 fl oz (60 ml) water

4 oz (110 g) chopped cooked onion

4 oz (110 g) minced cooked chicken

3 oz (80 g) canned tomatoes, drained weight, chopped

3 oz (80 g) hot, cooked rice

Mix curry powder, *garam masala* and chilli powder with the water. Add onion, chicken, chopped tomatoes and more water if too thick. Bring to boil and simmer for 10 minutes. Serve with hot rice.

Makes 1 serving

Chicken Tandoori

4 × 10 oz (110 g) skinned chicken portions

grated rind of 1 lemon

6 tablespoons lemon juice

2 teaspoons salt

1 teaspoon ground coriander

½ teaspoon cumin

1 teaspoon ground ginger

½ teaspoon garlic powder

2 tablespoons paprika

¼ teaspoon cayenne

10 fl oz (280 ml) natural unsweetened yogurt

1 tablespoon vinegar

lemon wedges for garnish

Skin chicken portions, make cuts at 1″ intervals about ½″ deep. Mix together lemon rind, 2 tablespoons lemon juice and salt. Rub into chicken flesh. Combine coriander, cumin, ginger, garlic, paprika and cayenne in a bowl and blend to a smooth paste with the remaining lemon juice. Stir in yogurt and vinegar. Spread over chicken portions. Cover with foil and allow to stand for 2 hours. Preheat oven to 400°F, Gas Mark 6, 200°C. Place portions on rack in roasting tin and cook in oven for 15 minutes. Spoon over the remaining marinade and return to oven. Reduce heat to 350°F, Gas Mark 4, 180°C. Bake for 1 hour or until chicken is cooked through. Increase temperature to 400°F, Gas Mark 6, 200°C for 15 minutes to brown. Garnish with lemon wedges and serve with salad. The flavour of this dish may be strengthened by marinating the raw chicken overnight.

Makes 4 servings

Cauliflower Poulet

2 lb (900 g) cauliflower

4 teaspoons cornflour

1 tablespoon dried onion flakes

1 pint (570 ml) chicken stock made with 1 cube

1 lb (460 g) cooked chicken, cubed

1 tablespoon curry powder or to taste

chopped parsley for garnish

Cook cauliflower in boiling, salted water until tender. Drain well and place half in a serving dish and keep hot. Turn remaining cauliflower into blender with the cornflour mixed with 4 tablespoons stock and blend until smooth. In a saucepan, bring remaining stock to the boil, add onion flakes and simmer until tender. Add blended cauliflower and cornflour, cubed chicken and curry powder, bring to the boil and simmer for 10 minutes. Pour over the cauliflower in serving dish, sprinkle with parsley, divide into 4 equal portions and serve at once.

Makes 4 servings

Braised Chicken in Foil

2 oz (60 g) onion

2 oz (60 g) tomatoes

2 oz (60 g) mushrooms

1 × 10 oz (280 g) skinned chicken leg

salt and pepper to taste

Preheat oven to 350°F, Gas Mark 4, 180°C. Slice onion, tomatoes and mushrooms onto a large piece of kitchen foil. Place chicken leg on vegetables and season to taste. Bring edges of foil together and fold over to seal, leaving plenty of air space in the 'parcel'. Cook in oven for approximately 1 hour.

Makes 1 serving

Chicken Goulash

1 clove garlic

salt

4 oz (110 g) onion, roughly chopped

10 fl oz (280 ml) chicken stock made with ½ cube

2 teaspoons paprika

4 teaspoons flour

1 tablespoon (½ oz, 15 g) tomato purée

salt and pepper to taste

12 oz (340 g) cooked chicken, cut in large pieces

1 sachet dried bouquet garni

3 oz (80 g) red pepper

6 oz (170 g) tomatoes

2½ fl oz (70 ml) natural unsweetened yogurt

Crush garlic with a good pinch of salt. Boil onion in a little of the stock until beginning to soften. Add paprika and cook for 1 minute. Add flour, tomato purée, garlic, salt and pepper and rest of stock and bring to the boil, stirring well. Add chicken pieces, *bouquet garni,* chopped red pepper. Cover and simmer very gently for 30 minutes. Peel tomatoes, cut into chunks and add to goulash. Simmer a few minutes longer. Turn into heated serving dish and stir in yogurt. Divide into 2 equal portions.

Makes 2 servings

Chicken and Peach Open Sandwich

1 slice bread (1 oz, 30 g)

1 teaspoon margarine

4 oz (110 g) cooked chicken, diced

1 medium peach

2 teaspoons mayonnaise

2½ fl oz (70 ml) natural unsweetened yogurt

2 teaspoons lemon juice

salt and pepper to taste

Toast bread and spread with margarine. Pile chicken on the toast. Dip peach in boiling water for 10 seconds, remove skin, cut peach in half and remove stone. Slice thinly and arrange slices over chicken. Mix mayonnaise with yogurt, lemon juice, salt and pepper. Pour over chicken and peach and serve with green salad.

Makes 1 serving

Poultry, Veal and Game

Spicy Marinated Chicken

2 × 6 oz (170 g) skinned chicken breasts

salt and pepper to taste

4 oz (110 g) onion

2 cloves garlic

1 teaspoon ground coriander

1 teaspoon garam masala

¼ teaspoon ground ginger

5 fl oz (140 ml) natural unsweetened yogurt

lemon and cress for garnish

Make slits in chicken flesh and prick with a fork. Sprinkle with salt. Put rest of ingredients, except lemon and cress, into blender and blend until smooth. Pour over chicken and leave to marinate for 1-2 hours. Preheat oven to 325°F, Gas Mark 3, 170°C. Line a baking tin with foil, place chicken in it with sauce and cover with foil. Bake for 30 minutes; uncover and cook for a further 30 minutes. Serve on a bed of green salad and garnish with lemon and cress.

Makes 2 servings

Turkey in Lemon and Mushroom Sauce

4 oz (110 g) chopped onion

3 oz (80 g) chopped mushrooms

1 tablespoon chopped parsley

juice and thinly peeled rind of ½ lemon

10 fl oz (280 ml) chicken stock made made with ½ cube

3 oz (80 g) chopped pickled cucumber

12 oz (340 g) diced, cooked turkey

3 teaspoons cornflour

1 oz (30 g) nonfat dry milk

Combine onion, mushroom, parsley, lemon rind and juice, chicken stock and pickled cucumber in a saucepan. Bring to the boil and simmer until vegetables are tender. Remove lemon rind, add turkey, bring back to the boil and simmer for a further 10 minutes. Mix cornflour with a little water, add to turkey mixture and cook until thickened. Remove from heat, add milk powder and stir until powder is completely dissolved. Divide into 2 equal portions and serve at once with green beans.

Makes 2 servings

Chicken Salad Medley

4 oz (110 g) cold cooked chicken, diced

1½ oz (45 g) red pepper, chopped

1½ oz (45 g) cucumber, chopped

4 oz (110 g) canned pineapple chunks, no sugar added

1 oz (30 g) onion, finely diced

3 oz (80 g) cooked rice

1 tablespoon mayonnaise

1 tablespoon lemon juice

½ teaspoon curry powder

In a salad bowl mix chicken, pepper, cucumber, pineapple, onion and rice. Mix mayonnaise, lemon juice and curry powder together. Pour over salad ingredients and toss together carefully. Serve lightly chilled.

Makes 1 serving

Turkey and Asparagus Mould

6 oz (170 g) canned asparagus, drained weight

½ chicken stock cube

3 teaspoons unflavoured gelatine

12 oz (340 g) cooked turkey

lettuce and watercress for garnish

When draining asparagus, reserve the liquid. Make liquid up to 10 fl oz (280 ml) with water. Add ½ stock cube and sprinkle in the gelatine. Heat gently in a small pan, stirring well. Do not allow mixture to boil. Cut turkey meat into small pieces. Arrange asparagus in a 1-pint mould, cover with chopped turkey and pour in the gelatine mixture. Leave in a cool place to set. Turn out and serve on a bed of lettuce and watercress. Divide into 2 equal portions.

Makes 2 servings

Left: Spicy Marinated Chicken

113

Poultry, Veal and Game

Chicken Chinese Style

12 oz (340 g) chicken meat

1 teaspoon salt

2 tablespoons soy sauce

6 oz (170 g) can bean sprouts

3 sticks celery, sliced

3 oz (80 g) button mushrooms, thinly sliced

8 oz (230 g) canned pineapple, no sugar added

5 fl oz (140 ml) chicken stock, made with ½ cube

2 teaspoons cornflour

salt and pepper to taste

6 oz (170 g) cooked crispy noodles*

Cut chicken meat into strips. Brown in non-stick pan for 3-5 minutes. Add salt and soy sauce. Add bean sprouts, celery, mushrooms, pineapple and stock. Cover and cook for 10 minutes. Blend cornflour with a little water, stir in, bring to boil and simmer until thickened. Season and serve with crispy noodles. Divide into 2 equal portions.

* Crispy Noodles:
Spread 6 oz (170 g) cooked noodles on baking tray and bake at top of hot oven, 400°F, Gas Mark 6, 200°C, until crispy and golden.

Makes 2 servings

Right: Chicken Chinese Style

114

Poultry, Veal and Game

Turkey Shepherd's Pie

4 oz (110 g) onion, finely chopped

1 teaspoon flour

2 tablespoons curry powder, or to taste

8 oz (230 g) canned tomatoes

4 teaspoons tomato ketchup

½ teaspoon salt

artificial sweetener to taste

2 medium cooking apples, peeled and finely chopped

12 oz (340 g) cooked turkey, chopped

6 oz (170 g) mashed potato

4 oz (110 g) frozen peas

Dry-fry onion, stir in flour and curry powder. Stir in tomatoes and tomato ketchup. Add salt and artificial sweetener and simmer gently for 30 minutes, stirring frequently to prevent burning. Add chopped apple and turkey, bring to the boil and simmer for 10 minutes until apple is just soft. Place on serving dish, pipe mashed potato round turkey mixture and arrange cooked peas down centre. Divide into 2 equal portions.

Makes 2 servings

Turkey Patties with Tomato Sauce

3 oz (80 g) mushrooms, finely chopped

1 teaspoon dried onion flakes

2 fl oz (60 ml) skim milk

4 oz (110 g) minced cooked turkey

1 slice bread (1 oz, 30g) made into crumbs

salt and pepper to taste

Tomato Sauce*

Put mushrooms, onion flakes and milk in a small saucepan and simmer gently for 3 minutes. Mix turkey, breadcrumbs, seasoning and mushroom mixture together. Cool. Form into 4 patties and grill turning once, until brown and thoroughly hot. Serve with 1 portion Tomato Sauce.

Makes 1 serving

*See p. 67 for sauce recipe

Indonesian Chicken

4 × 8 oz (230 g) skinned chicken joints

1 lb (460 g) onion, sliced

4 tablespoons soy sauce

juice of 2 lemons

1 pint (570 ml) tomato juice

2 teaspoons prepared mustard

½ teaspoon sambal oelek* or to taste

artificial sweetener to taste

12 oz (340 g) hot, cooked brown rice

Grill chicken or fry in dry non-stick pan until well browned. Dry-fry onions in non-stick pan, add remaining ingredients to chicken and onion and simmer over low heat for 45 minutes-1 hour or until tender. Divide into 4 equal portions. Divide rice evenly into 4 and serve with the chicken.

*Hot chilli seasoning.

Makes 4 servings

Shasliks of Lemon Chicken Tandoori

1 lb (460 g) skinned and boned chicken meat

2 lemons

1 clove garlic, crushed

½ teaspoon turmeric

sea salt to taste

6 oz (170 g) green pepper

6 oz (170 g) sweet red pepper

4 oz (110 g) onion

½ teaspoon grated nutmeg

For the rice:

3 oz (80 g) uncooked Basmati rice

10 fl oz (280 ml) chicken stock made from carcase (see p. 125)

Indian bouquet garni (onion flakes, garlic, cloves, cinnamon, cumin seed and coriander seed tied in muslin).

For the raita:

6 oz (170 g) tomatoes

3 oz (80 g) cucumber

5 fl oz (140 ml) natural unsweetened yogurt

Cut the chicken meat into ½″ thick strips. Make stock with carcase, chill, and remove fat before using. Remove peel from lemons as thinly as possible and cut peel into fine strips. Blanch in boiling water for 1 minute, drain and leave to dry. Combine lemon juice, garlic, turmeric and salt and roll chicken pieces in the mixture. Leave to marinate for at least 1 hour. Cut peppers into 1″ squares, slice onions, separate layers and cut into 1″ squares. Thread the skewers, alternating chicken, onion and peppers. Pack tightly and dust with freshly grated nutmeg. Cook under a hot grill for at least 20 minutes, turning skewers frequently. Cook rice in boiling stock with the *bouquet garni*. Drain well and weigh out two 3 oz portions. To make *raita*, skin and dice tomatoes and cucumber and fold into yogurt.

To serve, set portions of rice on individual plates and top with the skewers of cooked chicken and vegetables. Sprinkle liberally with the reserved strips of lemon peel. Serve *raita* separately and accompany with a green salad.

Makes 2 servings

Turkey Chilli

4 oz (110 g) onion, chopped

½ chicken stock cube

4 tablespoons water

8 fl oz (230 ml) Chilli Tomato Sauce*

½ teaspoon chilli seasoning

salt to taste

12 oz (340 g) cooked turkey, diced

6 oz (170 g) cooked elbow macaroni

In non-stick pan, cook onions with stock cube and water over low heat for 5 minutes, or until onions are tender but still crisp. Drain off water and add Chilli Tomato Sauce, chilli seasoning, salt, turkey and elbow macaroni. Bring to the boil and cook over low heat, stirring constantly for 10 minutes, or until thoroughly hot. Divide into 2 equal portions.

Makes 2 servings

*See p. 125 for sauce recipe

Turkey with Sweet and Sour Sauce

5 fl oz (140 ml) wine vinegar

12 oz (340 g) tomatoes, sliced

3 sticks celery, chopped

salt and pepper to taste

artificial sweetener to taste

½ teaspoon capers

12 oz (340 g) cooked turkey, cut into neat pieces

Put vinegar, sliced tomatoes, chopped celery, seasoning, sweetener and capers into a saucepan. Simmer for 10-15 minutes, add turkey, bring back to the boil and simmer for a further 10 minutes. Divide into 2 equal portions and serve with cauliflower.

Makes 2 servings

Jellied Chicken Mould

1 tablespoon unflavoured gelatine

1 chicken stock cube

5 fl oz (140 ml) water

salt and pepper

8 oz (230 g) cooked chicken

lettuce and tomato for garnish

Dissolve gelatine and stock cube in hot water, add salt and pepper to taste. Pour into blender and add chicken. Blend for 30 seconds. Divide evenly between two individual moulds and refrigerate until set. Turn out onto plates and garnish with lettuce and tomato.

Makes 2 servings

Left: Turkey with Sweet and Sour Sauce
Above: Jellied Chicken Mould

Poultry, Veal and Game

Roast Chicken with Garlic Sauce

1 × 2 lb (900 g) chicken

salt and black pepper to taste

12 cloves garlic

1 oz (30 g) nonfat dry milk

8 fl oz (230 ml) water

6 oz (170 g) fresh mushrooms, cut in half

1 teaspoon chopped parsley

⅛ teaspoon ground nutmeg

1 chicken stock cube

Preheat oven to 400°F, Gas Mark 6, 200°C. Season chicken with salt and pepper, wrap in foil, place in baking tin breast side down (this keeps the breast moist), and cook in oven for 1 hour. Boil garlic cloves in 3 changes of water, without salt. Drain. Dissolve dry skim milk in 8 fl oz water in a saucepan, add garlic, mushrooms, parsley, salt, black pepper, nutmeg and crumbled stock cube. Cook over low heat for 20 minutes. Transfer to a blender and run at medium speed until sauce is smooth. Skin chicken, weigh portions and serve with the sauce.

Makes 4 servings

Chicken Livers with Mushrooms

1 lb (460 g) chicken livers

6 oz (170 g) mushrooms

1 tablespoon dried onion flakes

15 fl oz (430 ml) chicken stock made with 1 cube

1 oz (30 g) nonfat dry milk

½ teaspoon curry powder

1 bay leaf

6 oz (170 g) green pepper

pinch dried oregano

salt and pepper to taste

Preheat oven to 400°F, Gas Mark 6, 200°C. Cook the chicken livers in a saucepan with water to cover until tender. Drain. Wash and slice the mushrooms. Stir onion flakes into the chicken stock and allow them to soften. Stir in the milk powder and curry powder. Arrange mushrooms in an ovenproof dish. Remove seeds and membranes from the pepper, slice thinly and place on top of the mushrooms. Distribute the chicken livers evenly over the sliced pepper. Add the bay leaf and oregano to the onion and curry sauce, adjust seasoning and pour over the chicken livers. Bake in oven for 20-25 minutes. Divide into 2 equal portions.

Makes 2 servings

Poultry, Veal and Game

Tomato Chicken Bake

4 tablespoons dried onion flakes

3 oz (80 g) button mushrooms, sliced

1½ oz (45 g) celery, chopped

3 oz (80 g) canned peppers, chopped

1 clove garlic, crushed

good pinch dried rosemary

pinch ground allspice

12 fl oz (340 ml) tomato juice

1 tablespoon lemon juice

4 × 10 oz (280 g) skinned chicken joints

salt and freshly ground black pepper

½ bunch watercress for garnish

Preheat oven to 325°F, Gas Mark 3, 170°C. Place the onion flakes in a saucepan with the mushrooms, celery, 2 tablespoons chopped peppers, garlic, rosemary, allspice and tomato juice. Bring to the boil, stirring occasionally and then simmer, uncovered, until the tomato juice is reduced by half. Stir in lemon juice. Cut each chicken joint in half and sprinkle with salt and pepper. Heat a non-stick frying pan and brown the chicken gently, turning frequently. Transfer to an ovenproof casserole. Spoon some of the tomato sauce over each portion. Bake for 35 minutes or until the chicken is tender. Baste with the tomato sauce every 10 minutes during cooking. Serve garnished with sprigs of watercress and the remaining peppers cut into thin strips.

Makes 4 servings

Turkey Pilaff

4 fl oz (110 ml) tomato juice

4 oz (110 g) cooked turkey, diced

3 oz (80 g) tomatoes, peeled and diced

2 oz (60 g) cooked diced onions

2 oz (60 g) cooked peas, drained weight

pinch mixed herbs

3 oz (80 g) cooked rice

salt and pepper to taste

Preheat oven to 375°F, Gas Mark 5, 190°C. Heat tomato juice gently in a saucepan, add remaining ingredients and mix well. Turn into a casserole and bake for about 30 minutes or until thoroughly hot. Serve with green salad.

Makes 1 serving

Piquant Tripe

2 lb (900 g) tripe, cut in strips

1¼ pints (750 ml) water

2 beef stock cubes

1 lemon, cut in slices

12 oz (340 g) green beans, halved

6 oz (170 g) carrots, sliced

3 oz (80 g) celery sticks, cut in 2″ lengths

8 teaspoons cornflour

2 tablespoons water

Combine tripe, water, stock cubes and lemon slices in a large saucepan. Cook covered, over low heat, for 1 hour. Add green beans, carrots and celery. Cook for about 20 minutes or until vegetables are tender. Mix cornflour with water, add to tripe, bring to the boil and cook for 2 minutes. Divide into 4 equal portions.

Makes 4 servings

Barbecued Chicken

6 × 10 oz (280 g) chicken joints, skinned

For the barbecue marinade:

8 fl oz (230 ml) wine vinegar

4 fl oz (110 ml) Worcester sauce

2 tablespoons dried onion flakes

1 teaspoon salt

1 teaspoon ground pepper

1 teaspoon dried marjoram

Place the chicken joints in a bowl. Combine all the marinade ingredients and pour over the chicken. Leave to marinate as long as possible, preferably overnight. Cook on a barbecue for about 40 minutes, basting occasionally with marinade during cooking. May also be cooked on a rack in a hot oven.

Makes 6 servings

Caribbean Chicken

2 × 10 oz (280 g) skinned chicken joints

2 oz (60 g) chopped onion

3 oz (80 g) green pepper

10 fl oz (280 ml) chicken stock made with ½ cube

2 teaspoons cornflour

2 rings canned pineapple, no sugar added, with 2 tablespoons juice

2 teaspoons tomato ketchup

2 teaspoons curry powder

salt and pepper to taste

1 medium banana

6 oz (170 g) hot cooked rice

Preheat oven to 350°F, Gas Mark 4, 180°C. Brown chicken joints in non-stick pan and then place in casserole dish. Brown onion and pepper and add to chicken. Blend cornflour with the pineapple juice, pour stock into the frying pan, add pineapple, cornflour and juice, ketchup, curry powder and seasoning. Bring to boil and pour over chicken. Bake in oven for 1 hour or until chicken is cooked. Peel banana, slice in half lengthwise, cut into pieces and stir into the sauce just before serving. Divide into 2 equal portions and serve with rice.

Makes 2 servings

Chicken Fricassee

1 oz (30 g) nonfat dry milk

5 oz (140 g) cottage cheese

4 oz (110 g) cooked chicken

1 tablespoon dried onion flakes

4 oz (110 g) canned peas, drained weight

salt, pepper and chicken barbecue seasoning to taste

2 slices bread (2 oz, 60 g), toasted

parsley for garnish

Make dry milk powder up to 5 fl oz (140 ml) with water. Mix with cottage cheese and rub through sieve or blend in electric blender. Dice chicken and place in a pan with the cheese mixture, onion flakes and peas. Season to taste and simmer gently for 15 minutes, stirring with a wooden spoon. Sprinkle with chicken barbecue seasoning and serve with triangles of toast and a green vegetable. Garnish with parsley and divide into 2 equal portions.

Makes 2 servings

Left: Caribbean Chicken

Poultry, Veal and Game

Veal Oriental

1½ lbs (700 g) minced veal

salt and pepper to taste

4 oz (110 g) onion, sliced and finely chopped

3 oz (80 g) carrot, grated

3 oz (80 g) mushrooms, finely sliced

12 oz (340 g) canned pineapple chunks, no sugar added

6 teaspoons tomato ketchup

3 teaspoons vinegar

3 teaspoons soy sauce

6 oz (170 g) green pepper, finely chopped

10 fl oz (280 ml) chicken stock made with 1 cube

artificial sweetener to taste

3 teaspoons arrowroot

9 oz (260 g) hot cooked rice

Season veal, dip hands in water, roll meat into small balls and then drop gently into boiling, salted water. Cook for approximately 10 minutes and remove with slotted spoon. In a saucepan, mix together onion, carrots, mushrooms, pineapple, tomato ketchup, vinegar, soy sauce, chopped pepper, chicken stock, sweetener and salt and pepper to taste. Cook over moderate heat for approximately 30 minutes. Mix arrowroot with 1 tablespoon water, add to vegetable mixture and cook until thickened. Add veal balls, return to the boil and simmer for 10 minutes. Divide meat, sauce and rice into 3 equal portions before serving.

Makes 3 servings

Fricassee of Veal

2 lbs (900 g) boneless stewing veal

1 pint (570 ml) water

salt

1 bayleaf

6 white peppercorns

4 oz (110 g) onions or shallots

6 cloves

Sauce:

1 pint (570 ml) stock made with 1 cube

6 teaspoons flour

2-3 sprigs fresh dill, finely chopped

1 tablespoon vinegar

artificial sweetener to taste

6 oz (170 g) button mushrooms

1 tablespoon lemon juice

12 oz (340 g) cooked new potatoes

Cut meat into large pieces. Place in a saucepan, add water and bring to the boil. Skim, then add spices and the onions studded with cloves. Simmer for 1-1½ hours or until meat is tender. Cool. Strain off liquid and discard. Take out onions, remove cloves and chop onions. Heat stock. Mix flour with a little water, add to stock and boil for 1 minute. Add dill, vinegar, sweetener, mushrooms, lemon juice and the chopped cooked onions. Add cooked meat to the sauce and reheat gently for 15 minutes. Serve with new potatoes and a salad of lettuce, cucumber and tomatoes. Divide into 4 equal portions.

Makes 4 servings

Polish Stew

1 lb (460 g) boned rabbit, cut into dice

6 oz (170 g) white cabbage, finely chopped

6 oz (170 g) sauerkraut, finely chopped

12 oz (340 g) canned tomatoes

8 oz (230 g) onions, diced

3 oz (80 g) mushrooms, sliced

3 oz (80 g) carrots, diced

4 teaspoons caraway seeds

2 tablespoons (1 oz, 30 g) tomato purée

10 fl oz (280 ml) water

2 teaspoons paprika

½ teaspoon ground bay leaves

1 clove garlic, crushed

salt and pepper to taste

Preheat oven to 375°F, Gas Mark 5, 190°C. Place rabbit pieces in thick-based saucepan sprinkled with a little salt. Brown and transfer to 4-pint casserole. Arrange cabbage, sauerkraut, tomatoes, onions, mushrooms and carrots over meat. Sprinkle with caraway seeds. Mix tomato purée with water, add paprika, ground bay leaves, crushed garlic, salt and pepper to taste. Mix well, pour over contents of casserole, cover with a lid or foil and cook in oven for 1½-2 hours, or until rabbit and vegetables are tender. Serve piping hot. Divide into 2 equal portions.

Makes 2 servings

Indian Veal with Rice

8 oz (230 g) veal steak, without bone

3 oz (80 g) celery, finely chopped

1 medium apple, peeled, cored and chopped

salt and pepper to taste

1-2 teaspoons curry powder, or to taste

pinch ground ginger

1½ fl oz (45ml) buttermilk or 1½ fl oz (45 ml) natural unsweetened yogurt

3 oz (80 g) hot cooked rice

Cut meat into cubes. Dry-fry in non-stick pan until browned. Remove veal to a plate, wipe pan clean and return to stove. Return meat to pan and add finely chopped celery and apple. Add salt, pepper, curry powder and ground ginger. Add about 2 tablespoons water, cover and cook for 10-15 minutes. When cooked stir in buttermilk or yogurt. Serve with rice.

Makes 1 serving

Chicken Stock

1 chicken carcase

2 pints (1 litre 140 ml) water

1 stick celery, with leaves

3 oz (80 g) carrots

1 clove garlic

3 peppercorns

1 bay leaf

⅛ teaspoon thyme

salt to taste

Place chicken carcase in a large saucepan with the water. Chop celery roughly, slice carrots and crush garlic. Add to the pan with the herbs and salt. Bring to the boil and simmer gently for 1½ hours. Strain to remove solids. Cool stock quickly and place in refrigerator until fat congeals on top. Skim off fat and discard. Divide stock into 6 fl oz (170 ml) portions. (6 fl oz is equivalent to 1 serving bouillon or stock).

Sauces for Poultry

Bread Sauce

10 fl oz (280 ml) skim milk

large pinch ground cloves

¼ teaspoon salt

freshly ground pepper

1 teaspoon dried onion flakes

4 slices bread (4 oz, 110 g) made into crumbs

Put milk in a saucepan with ground cloves, salt, pepper and onion flakes. Bring to boil and simmer until onion is softened. Stir in the breadcrumbs and mix well. Simmer for a further 3-4 minutes. Serve with chicken or turkey. Divide evenly.

Makes 4 servings

Cranberry Sauce

1¼ lb (570 g) cranberries

5 fl oz (140 ml) water

artificial sweetener to taste

1 oz (30 g) nonfat dry milk

Cook the cranberries in the water until they pop open, mash and add sweetener to taste. Add dry milk to modify the sourness of the cranberries. Turn into screw-top jar and store in refrigerator. Excellent with poultry or other meats. Divide evenly.

Makes 4 servings

Tasty Stuffing

4 slices bread (4 oz, 110 g) made into crumbs

3 oz (80 g) green pepper

3 sticks celery

1 tablespoon dried thyme

1 teaspoon finely grated lemon rind

2 tablespoons dried onion flakes

salt and pepper

2 fl oz (60 ml) skim milk

Remove seeds and membranes from green pepper and chop finely. Chop celery finely. Mix with the breadcrumbs and the thyme, lemon rind, onion flakes, salt and pepper. Add skim milk to bind into a stiff mixture. Use for stuffing fish or bake in the oven and serve with chicken. Divide evenly.

Makes 4 servings

Chilli Tomato Sauce

16 fl oz (460 ml) tomato juice

1 tablespoon lemon juice

artificial sweetener to taste

½ teaspoon chilli seasoning

¼ teaspoon salt

¼ teaspoon pepper

Combine all ingredients in saucepan, simmer uncovered for 20 minutes or until mixture is reduced by half. Store in screw-top jars in refrigerator. Delicious with poultry, meat or fish.

Makes 4 servings

Desserts

Yes, you *can* eat desserts while learning how to lose weight! If that last course in a meal has been your downfall in the past, try some of these delicious recipes. You will soon see just one of the reasons why the Weight Watchers Programme is so successful – you can stay on it for life without ever having to give up that taste of 'something sweet'. Fruits are the mainstay of light, flavoursome desserts, and they combine perfectly with items from your milk allowance such as skim milk and yogurt. Unflavoured gelatine, arrowroot or cornflour may be included in permitted amounts for set or moulded desserts. And by skilful use of your allowances of bread and flour you can also enjoy some of the more substantial puddings from time to time. To make desserts appealing to the eye, use individual dishes, or tall glasses for sorbets and ices. Top with a sprinkling of spice or a twist of peel, or reserve a few whole berries for decoration.

Desserts

Alpine Dessert

1 tablespoon unflavoured gelatine
2 tablespoons cold water
4 tablespoons boiling water
10 fl oz (280 ml) natural unsweetened yogurt
10 oz (280 g) curd cheese
artificial sweetener to taste
10 oz (280 g) raspberries

Cover gelatine with 2 tablespoons cold water, allow to swell, add boiling water and stir until dissolved. Place yogurt, curd cheese, sweetener and dissolved gelatine in the blender. Blend until well mixed. Pour into basin and fold in 8 oz (230 g) of the raspberries. Divide mixture evenly between 4 dessert bowls. Decorate with remaining raspberries. Put in a cool place to set.

Makes 4 servings

Banana Bread

1 teaspoon baking powder
¼ teaspoon bicarbonate of soda
6 teaspoons self-raising flour
¼ teaspoon salt
2 slices white bread (2 oz, 60 g) made into fine crumbs
2 standard eggs
3 teaspoons vegetable oil
artificial sweetener to taste
1 very ripe medium banana, mashed

Preheat oven to 350°F, Gas Mark 4, 180°C. Sift baking powder, soda, flour and salt into breadcrumbs. Beat together eggs, oil and sweetener. Add flour mixture and mashed banana alternately to the egg mixture. Line a 1″ deep baking tin with foil or greaseproof paper, pour in mixture. Bake in oven for 45 minutes, or until bread springs back when lightly pressed with finger. Divide into 2 equal portions.

Makes 2 servings

Mandarin Chocolate Dessert Cake

2 slices bread (2 oz, 60 g) made into crumbs
5 fl oz (140 ml) lukewarm water
2 standard eggs, separated
2 teaspoons chocolate Colour Flavouring
1 oz (30 g) nonfat dry milk
1 teaspoon unsweetened cocoa powder
artificial sweetener to taste
8 oz (230 g) mandarin orange sections, no sugar added

Icing

6 teaspoons margarine
1 oz (30 g) nonfat dry milk
2 teaspoons unsweetened cocoa powder
1 teaspoon chocolate Colour Flavouring
1 teaspoon instant coffee, dissolved in 1 teaspoon hot water

Preheat oven to 375°F, Gas Mark 5, 190°C. In large basin put breadcrumbs, water, egg yolks, chocolate Colour Flavouring, dry milk, cocoa and sweetener. Beat together thoroughly. Whip egg whites until stiff peaks form, fold carefully into breadcrumb mixture. Pour into 9″ cake tin and bake for 25-30 minutes. Remove from oven, turn out onto wire rack and allow to cool completely.

For icing: mix all ingredients together and chill in refrigerator. Slice cake through middle and spread half the icing over the base. Drain orange sections throroughly and use half to decorate the outer edge of the cake base. Cover with other half of cake. Spread rest of icing on top and decorate with remaining oranges. Chill in refrigerator and divide into 2 equal portions before serving.

NB To pipe a design onto the cake, leave icing in refrigerator for several hours then, using forcing bag, decorate in any way desired.

Makes 2 servings

Apple and Orange Crisp

12 oz (340 g) canned apple, no sugar added
10 fl oz (280 ml) natural unsweetened yogurt
1 teaspoon cinnamon
artificial sweetener to taste
4 slices bread (4 oz, 110 g) made into crumbs
4 teaspoons margarine
1 medium orange, sliced

Heat apple, blend in yogurt, cinnamon and sweetener. Spread breadcrumbs on grill pan and toast gently, shaking occasionally, until crisp. Mix crumbs with margarine and a few drops of sweetener. Spoon breadcrumbs and apple into a glass dish in alternate layers, ending with a layer of apple. Decorate with sliced orange and chill. Divide into 4 equal portions before serving.

Makes 4 servings

Right: Mandarin Chocolate Dessert Cake

Desserts

Blackcurrant Cheesecake

4 slices brown bread (4 oz, 110 g) made into crumbs

4 tablespoons margarine

½ teaspoon cinnamon

1 tablespoon unflavoured gelatine

2 tablespoons hot water

1¼ lbs (570 g) curd cheese

grated lemon rind

artificial sweetener to taste

11 oz (310 g) fresh blackcurrants

4 teaspoons arrowroot

1 oz (30 g) fresh redcurrants for garnish

Spread breadcrumbs on grill pan and toast gently, shaking pan occasionally, until crisp and golden brown. In a basin mix crumbs thoroughly with the margarine and cinnamon. Turn into loose-bottomed 6″ cake tin, press mixture over base of tin, put in refrigerator until well chilled. Dissolve gelatine in 2 tablespoons hot water, beat into curd cheese, adding lemon rind and sweetener to taste. Spread over crumb base and chill until set. Bring blackcurrants to the boil in a small pan with a little water. Cook for 2-3 minutes until soft. Mix arrowroot to thin paste with water, add to fruit and continue cooking, stirring all the time, until thickened. Allow to cool and then spread over cheese mixture. Chill cake thoroughly before removing from tin. Garnish with redcurrants, divide evenly into 4 portions.

Makes 4 servings

Apricot Whip

4 ripe medium apricots, stoned

10 fl oz (280 ml) natural unsweetened yogurt

artificial sweetener to taste

¼ teaspoon lemon flavouring

few drops apricot flavouring

1 tablespoon unflavoured gelatine

4 tablespoons water

Put half the fruit in blender. Add yogurt, sweetener and flavouring. Sprinkle gelatine over water in small saucepan, let stand to soften. Stir over low heat until gelatine is dissolved. Add to fruit mixture and blend until smooth. Remove blender goblet from the machine and chill for a few minutes in refrigerator. Replace on machine and blend until mixture thickens. Dice remainder of fruit and fold into the mixture. Divide evenly between 2 dessert glasses. Chill well before serving.

Makes 2 servings

Berrie Jelly

6 oz (170 g) gooseberries

6 oz (170 g) raspberries

4 tablespoons undiluted low-calorie orange drink

artificial sweetener to taste

6 teaspoons unflavoured gelatine

cold water

Put first 4 ingredients into saucepan and simmer gently until fruit is soft. Add gelatine and stir until dissolved. Make up to 15 fl oz (430 ml) with cold water and then turn into a mould, rinsed with cold water. Chill in refrigerator until set, and divide into 4 equal portions before serving.

Makes 4 servings

Caribbean Sorbet

3 teaspoons unflavoured gelatine

8 tablespoons warm water

2 tablespoons undiluted low-calorie lemon drink

2 tablespoons undiluted low-calorie lime drink

5 fl oz (140 ml) natural unsweetened yogurt

1 standard egg white

2 canned pineapple rings, no sugar added, with 2 tablespoons juice

Dissolve the gelatine in 4 table-spoons warm water. Combine the fruit drinks and remaining water in basin, add gelatine and pineapple juice and stir. Stir in yogurt. Chill until lightly set and then whisk well. Whisk egg white until stiff and fold into the mixture. Freeze in a suitable container. When required, thaw slightly and garnish with the pineapple slices.

NB When this dessert is used, the egg yolk must be eaten at the same meal.

Makes 1 serving

Finnish Apple Dessert

4 medium cooking apples

8 medium prunes, soaked

artificial sweetener to taste

4 portions Weight Watchers Frozen Vanilla Dessert

Preheat oven to 375°F, Gas Mark 5, 190°C. Core apples and make an incision round the centre of each. Stone and chop prunes and use to stuff the apples. Place in ovenproof casserole, sprinkle with sweetener, cover and bake for 1-1½ hours. Place apples in 4 individual dishes and serve with portions of Weight Watchers Frozen Vanilla Dessert.

Makes 4 servings

Cold Apricot Soufflé

'Cream'

1 teaspoon unflavoured gelatine

5 fl oz (140 ml) water

2-3 drops almond flavouring

artificial sweetener to taste

1 oz (30 g) nonfat dry milk

Warm half the water and dissolve gelatine in it. Add remaining water and rest of ingredients. Stir well and leave to set.

Soufflé

2 standard eggs, separated

artificial sweetener to taste

2 teaspoons cornflour

10 fl oz (280 ml) skim milk

4 teaspoons unflavoured gelatine

3 tablespoons water

2-3 drops vanilla flavouring

4 medium apricots, cooked and stoned

Beat egg yolks with sweetener and cornflour until thick and light in colour. Bring milk to boil and add to egg mixture, stirring constantly. Return mixture to pan and stir over low heat until custard coats back of spoon. Do not let it boil. Dissolve gelatine in water over low heat. Mix well with the egg mixture and add vanilla flavouring. Cool. When mixture is on point of setting, whip the 'cream' until thick and fluffy and carefully add to custard. Whisk egg whites until stiff and fold into mixture. Put cooked, stoned apricots in blender and blend until smooth. Pour over base of 3-pint soufflé dish, add soufflé mixture, put in refrigerator to set. Divide into 2 equal portions.

Makes 2 servings

Banana Split

5 fl oz (140 ml) skim milk

3 teaspoons unsweetened cocoa powder

2 teaspoons chocolate Colour Flavouring

3 teaspoons cornflour

artificial sweetener to taste

1 medium banana

lemon juice

2 portions Weight Watchers Frozen Vanilla Dessert

Using a double saucepan or a small pan over boiling water, make chocolate sauce by whisking milk, cocoa, chocolate Colour Flavouring, cornflour and sweetener together until hot and thick. Split banana lengthwise, brush with lemon juice to prevent discoloration. Using a scoop, put two portions of Weight Watchers Frozen Vanilla Dessert in rounds between banana halves. Pour over hot chocolate sauce, divide into 2 equal portions and serve immediately.

Makes 2 servings

Apple Dessert Cake

*2 slices bread (2 oz, 60 g)
made into crumbs*

5 fl oz (140 ml) skim milk

*4 oz (110 g) canned apple, no sugar
added*

2 standard eggs

2 teaspoons lemon juice

grated rind of ½ lemon

artificial sweetener to taste

*2 portions Weight Watchers Frozen
Vanilla Dessert*

Preheat oven to 350°F, Gas Mark 4, 180°C. Pour milk over breadcrumbs in a basin and leave to soak. Roughly chop apple, separate eggs and beat whites until stiff peaks form. Beat yolks until creamy. Add breadcrumbs, apple, lemon juice, rind and artificial sweetener and beat thoroughly. Fold in egg whites. Turn mixture gently to distribute whites evenly. Pour mixture into a deep 6″ cake tin. Bake for 35-40 minutes until cake is well risen and golden brown and springs back if pressed lightly with finger. Turn out onto cake tray to cool. Divide into 2 equal portions and serve each with a portion of Weight Watchers Frozen Vanilla Dessert.

Makes 2 servings

Peach Melba

1 medium peach

2 tablespoons hot water

artificial sweetener to taste

3 oz (80 g) fresh raspberries

*1 portion Weight Watchers Frozen
Vanilla Dessert*

Skin and halve peach, removing stone. Poach halves very gently for about 7 minutes in hot water with sweetener, turning carefully from time to time. Meanwhile, press raspberries through a fine sieve and discard seeds. Shape Vanilla Dessert into rounds and place in dessert glass with the peach halves. Top with raspberry purée. Serve at once.

Makes 1 serving

*Left : Apple Dessert Cake
Above : Peach Melba*

Desserts

Cottage Cheesecake

4 slices bread (4 oz, 110 g)

10 oz (280 g) cottage cheese

4 standard eggs

10 fl oz (280 ml) skim milk

artificial sweetener to taste

8 teaspoons low-calorie marmalade

1 lemon

Pre heat oven to 450°F, Gas Mark 8, 230°C. Bake bread until golden brown. Crush the bread with a rolling pin to make it into crumbs. Spread them over the base of an 8″ spring-form tin.

Reduce oven heat to 350°F, Gas Mark 4, 180°C. Rub the cottage cheese through a metal sieve or beat in an electric mixer at a very high speed. Add the eggs, milk, artificial sweetener and the finely grated rind and juice of the lemon. Mix thoroughly. When smooth, pour the cheese mixture over the crumbs in the cake tin. Bake for 30-40 minutes or until set. Spread marmalade over top, place cheesecake in the refrigerator and chill overnight. Remove from tin, divide into 4 equal portions and serve.

Makes 4 servings.

Early Summer Pudding

12 oz (340 g) blackcurrants

water

artificial sweetener to taste

4 teaspoons margarine

4 slices white bread (4 oz, 110 g)

Put blackcurrants in a saucepan and add water to come halfway up the fruit. Bring to the boil and cook for 1-2 minutes. Add sweetener to taste. Meanwhile, spread bread with margarine and cut the slices to fit round a 1-pint basin, leaving a piece to make a 'lid'. Pour in the fruit and fit remaining bread over it. Cover with a saucer and top with a weight. Chill well. Divide into 4 equal portions and serve with Custard Sauce*.

Makes 4 servings

*See p. 143 for sauce recipe

Pineapple Mousse

2 tablespoons hot water

3 teaspoons unflavoured gelatine

10 fl oz (280 ml) skim milk, warmed

4 oz (110 g) canned crushed pineapple, no sugar added

artificial sweetener to taste

Pour hot water into blender goblet, sprinkle in gelatine and blend until mixed. Add the warmed milk and blend again. Add crushed pineapple and sweetener to taste and blend until smooth. Turn into a dish to set. Chill well and divide into 2 equal portions.

Makes 2 servings

Desserts

Blackcurrant and Raspberry Dessert

1 medium orange

¼ teaspoon cinnamon

artificial sweetener to taste

3 teaspoons cornflour

5 fl oz (140 ml) water

3 oz (80 g) blackcurrants, fresh or frozen

3 oz (80 g) raspberries, fresh or frozen

Using a sharp knife or vegetable peeler, peel thin strips of orange peel for decoration. Squeeze orange and reserve the juice. Blend cornflour with 2 tablespoons water. Add remaining water, cinnamon, sweetener and orange juice. Stir in blackcurrants and raspberries and cook until juice is slightly thickened and fruit is soft but not broken. When slightly cooled, divide evenly between 3 individual glasses and serve chilled, garnished with orange peel.

Makes 3 servings

Mock Cream

2½ oz (70 g) curd cheese

artificial sweetener to taste

2-3 drops vanilla flavouring

3 tablespoons skim milk, or more if required

Beat all ingredients together thoroughly and use over a chosen serving of fruit.

Makes 1 serving

Whipped Topping

½ oz (15 g) nonfat dry milk

½ teaspoon lemon juice

¼ teaspoon vanilla flavouring

1 tablespoon water

artificial sweetener to taste

Combine all ingredients in bowl and beat together for about 5 minutes, or until mixture stands in peaks. Divide into 2 equal portions. May be served with any chosen dessert.

Makes 2 servings

Peach Mousse

3 teaspoons unflavoured gelatine

4 tablespoons water

8 oz (230 g) sliced peaches, no sugar added

10 fl oz (280 g) natural, unsweetened yogurt

artificial sweetener to taste

Dissolve gelatine in hot water. Place all ingredients in blender and blend until smooth. Divide evenly between 2 dishes and put in refrigerator until set.

Makes 2 servings

Coffee Yogurt

1 teaspoon instant coffee

5 fl oz (140 ml) natural, unsweetened yogurt

artificial sweetener to taste

Mix coffee with 2 teaspoons hot water, add to yogurt in small bowl. Mix thoroughly and chill before serving.

Makes 1 serving

Rum and Pineapple Yogurt

5 fl oz (140 ml) natural, unsweetened yogurt

artificial sweetener to taste

few drops yellow food colouring

4 oz (110 g) canned, crushed pineapple, no sugar added

few drops rum flavouring

Mix all ingredients together and chill.

Makes 1 serving

Rum and Banana Yogurt

As above, using ½ medium banana instead of pineapple.

Makes 1 serving

Chocolate Yogurt

5 fl oz (140 ml) natural, unsweetened yogurt

artificial sweetener to taste

1 teaspoon unsweetened cocoa powder, dissolved in a little hot water

Mix all ingredients together and chill.

Makes 1 serving

Yogurt Orange Sorbet

10 fl oz (280 ml)
natural unsweetened yogurt

4 fl oz (110 ml) canned orange
juice, no sugar added

2 medium oranges

1 tablespoon unflavoured gelatine

4 tablespoons water

2 standard egg whites

Turn refrigerator to coldest setting. Grate the zest from the oranges and combine with the yogurt and orange juice in a bowl. Dissolve the gelatine in the water over low heat and add to the yogurt mixture. In a separate bowl, whisk the egg whites until stiff peaks form. When gelatine mixture begins to set, fold in beaten egg whites, pour into a shallow dish and freeze. To serve, remove remaining peel and pith from the fresh oranges and slice them. Divide sorbet mixture and orange slices evenly between 2 sundae glasses, finishing with a layer of orange slices.

NB When this dessert is used, the egg yolk must be eaten at the same meal.

Makes 2 servings

Right: Yogurt Orange Sorbet
Far right: Strawberry Pancake
with Orange Sauce

136

Strawberry Pancake with Orange Sauce

1 standard egg

1 slice bread (1 oz, 30 g) made into crumbs

2½ fl oz (70 ml) skim milk

Sauce:

juice and grated rind of ½ orange

3 teaspoons margarine

⅛ teaspoon brandy flavouring

artificial sweetener to taste

2½ oz (70 g) strawberries, sliced

First, make the sauce. In a small saucepan, cook the orange rind in the orange juice until tender. Remove pan from heat and stir in margarine, flavouring and sweetener. Stir until well mixed and keep warm. Place egg, breadcrumbs and milk in blender and blend until smooth and creamy. Gently heat a 7″ non-stick pan, pour in the mixture and twist pan so that the base is evenly covered. Cook until underside is set. With a spatula, gently loosen the pancake and turn it over to cook the other side. Slide carefully onto a warm plate. Arrange sliced strawberries on the pancake, fold over and serve with the sauce.

Makes 1 serving

Desserts

Tangy Apple Dessert

2 medium cooking apples

8 tablespoons water

4 teaspoons cornflour

juice and rind of 1 lemon

artificial sweetener to taste

mint and lemon peel for garnish

Peel, core and slice apples and stew in 4 tablespoons water. In a small pan, mix cornflour with remaining water, add finely grated lemon rind and juice and cook gently until thick, stirring constantly. Add stewed apples and sweetener to taste and mix well. Cool and divide evenly between 2 sundae glasses. Chill well and decorate with sprigs of mint and a twist of lemon peel. Divide into 2 equal portions.

Makes 2 servings

Rhubarb Fool

9 oz (260 g) rhubarb

rind and juice of 1 medium orange

artificial sweetener to taste

5 fl oz (140ml) natural unsweetened yogurt

2 portions Weight Watchers Frozen Vanilla Dessert

Preheat oven to 350°F, Gas Mark 4, 180°C. Cut the rhubarb into small pieces and put in ovenproof dish. Add rind and juice of orange and bake for 15 minutes or until tender. Turn into blender goblet and blend until smooth. Add sweetener to taste. Fold in yogurt. Divide evenly between 2 individual dessert dishes. Serve chilled with Weight Watchers Frozen Vanilla Dessert.

Makes 2 servings

Cheesy Pineapple Pudding

4 slices canned pineapple, no sugar added, with 4 tablespoons juice

2 standard eggs

4 fl oz (110 ml) skim milk

½ teaspoon vanilla flavouring

artificial sweetener to taste

5 oz (140 g) cottage cheese

6 oz (170 g) cooked rice

cinnamon to taste

Preheat oven to 375°F, Gas Mark 5, 190°C. Chop pineapple, mix all ingredients thoroughly except cinnamon. Pour into 2-pint baking dish, sprinkle with cinnamon. Bake for 30-40 minutes or until knife comes out clean when inserted into centre of pudding. Divide into 2 equal portions. May be served warm or chilled.

Makes 2 servings

Desserts

Prune Mousse

8 medium dried prunes

5 fl oz (140 ml) water

artificial sweetener to taste

10 fl oz (280 ml) natural unsweetened yogurt

1 tablespoon unflavoured gelatine

Soak prunes overnight. Simmer in water for 10 minutes, add sweetener and allow to cool. Remove prunes, reserving cooking liquid. Stone the prunes and put into blender, reserving one for decoration. Add yogurt, reserving 1 tablespoon for decoration, and blend until well mixed. Dissolve gelatine in cooking liquid. Add to rest of ingredients. Blend for a few seconds until well mixed. Turn into mould and leave until set. Turn out onto serving dish and decorate with yogurt and remaining prune. Divide into 2 equal portions.

Makes 2 servings

Pear Chocolate Cake with Swiss Cream

4 small pears, cored, peeled and sliced

2 oz (60 g) nonfat dry milk

10 fl oz (280 ml) skim milk

4 slices bread (4 oz, 110 g) made into crumbs

2 tablespoons unsweetened cocoa powder

artificial sweetener to taste

1 teaspoon baking powder

Swiss Cream:

10 fl oz (280 ml) natural, unsweetened yogurt

½ teaspoon crème de menthe *Colour Flavouring*

artificial sweetener to taste

Preheat oven to 375°F, Gas Mark 5, 190°C. Mix all cake ingredients in blender until puréed. Pour into shallow non-stick baking tin and bake for 1 hour. Cool and refrigerate for 2-3 hours. To make Swiss Cream, combine all ingredients in a basin and mix thoroughly. Spoon over cake. Divide cake into 4 equal portions.

Makes 4 servings

Peach Delight

1 medium peach

1 teaspoon margarine

3 teaspoons flour

artificial sweetener to taste

2 drops almond flavouring

4 tablespoons low-calorie orange drink, diluted with 4 tablespoons water

2 drops brandy flavouring

1 portion Weight Watchers Frozen Vanilla Dessert

Skin and halve the peach and remove stone. Mix margarine, flour, artificial sweetener and almond flavouring to form a paste. Replace stone with paste, put the peach halves together and secure with wooden cocktail sticks. Place in small pan with the orange drink, water and brandy flavouring. Poach gently over low heat for 20-30 minutes, turning occasionally. Serve hot with Weight Watchers Frozen Vanilla Dessert.

Makes 1 serving

Steamed Chocolate Pudding with Chocolate Sauce

4 standard eggs, separated

6 tablespoons water

2 teaspoons chocolate Colour Flavouring

2 teaspoons unsweetened cocoa powder

1 teaspoon instant coffee powder

artificial sweetener to taste

¼ teaspoon vanilla flavouring

4 slices brown bread (4 oz, 110 g), made into crumbs

8 teaspoons self-raising flour

2 oz (60 g) nonfat dry milk

Put egg yolks in a mixing bowl, add water, chocolate Colour Flavouring, cocoa, coffee, sweetener and vanilla flavouring. Whip until frothy. Add breadcrumbs, flour and dry milk and mix thoroughly. Beat egg whites until stiff peaks form. Carefully fold egg whites into yolk mixture and pour into basin. Cover tightly with foil, place in steamer and steam for 1½ hours. Divide into 4 equal portions and serve with Chocolate Sauce.*

Makes 4 servings

*See p. 143 for sauce recipe.

Strawberry 'Cream'

*10 fl oz (280 ml) natural
unsweetened yogurt*

1 oz (30 g) nonfat dry milk

4 teaspoons unflavoured gelatine

*10 oz (280 g) fresh or frozen
strawberries*

artificial sweetener to taste

Put yogurt, dry milk and gelatine in
blender and blend for about 30
seconds. Add strawberries,
reserving some for decoration, add
sweetener and blend again. Pour
into a glass dish and chill in
refrigerator for 1 hour. Decorate
with remaining strawberries and
divide into 2 equal portions before
serving.

Makes 2 servings

Above: Strawberry "Cream"
Right: Pineapple Sponge Custard

Pineapple Sponge Custard

6 teaspoons self-raising flour

artificial sweetener to taste

juice and rind of 1 small lemon

2 standard eggs

5 fl oz (140 ml) skim milk

*4 slices canned pineapple, no sugar
added, with 4 tablespoons juice*

Preheat oven to 350°F, Gas Mark 4,
180°C. In a large bowl, mix flour,
the sweetener, pineapple juice,
lemon juice, rind, egg yolks, and
milk, stirring all the time. Whisk egg
whites until stiff and slowly fold into
liquid mixture using a wooden
spoon. reserving 1 slice of pineapple
for garnish, cut remainder into $\frac{1}{2}''$
pieces and arrange in the base
of a 1-pint soufflé dish. Gently pour
egg mixture over the fruit. Put dish
in a deep baking tin, add hot water to
come 1″ up the sides of the dish and
bake for 55 minutes, or until golden
brown and firm to the touch.
Decorate with pieces of pineapple.
Divide into 2 equal portions and
serve at once.

Makes 2 servings

Desserts

Cranberry-Pineapple Dessert

10 oz (280 g) cranberries

artificial sweetener to taste

⅛ teaspoon orange flavouring

16 fl oz (460 ml) water

4 slices canned pineapple, no sugar added, with 4 tablespoons juice

1 tablespoon unflavoured gelatine

1 teaspoon lemon juice

Combine first 4 ingredients in blender and blend for 20 seconds. Transfer to saucepan and simmer slowly for about 15 minutes or until mixture thickens. Strain through a fine sieve and return to saucepan. Chop pineapple and add to the pan with the pineapple juice, gelatine and lemon juice. Stir all together over very low heat until gelatine is dissolved. Turn into a serving dish and chill. Divide into 4 equal portions.

Makes 4 servings

Lemon Fluff

2 standard eggs, separated

4 teaspoons cornflour

juice of 2 lemons

rind of 1 lemon

1 tablespoon unflavoured gelatine

10 fl oz (280 ml) water

pinch cream of tartar

artificial sweetener to taste

12 medium black grapes

sprigs of mint for garnish

Place egg yolks, cornflour, lemon juice and rind in the top half of a double saucepan over boiling water and beat well until mixture begins to thicken. Remove from the heat. Dissolve gelatine in the water in a small pan over low heat. Beat into the lemon mixture. Whisk egg whites with cream of tartar until frothy. Add sweetener to taste. Fold egg whites into lemon mixture and divide evenly between 2 individual dishes. Chill until set. Serve topped with grapes and garnished with sprigs of mint.

Makes 2 servings

Grapefruit and Orange Dessert

2 tablespoons unflavoured gelatine

4 tablespoons hot water

4 fl oz (110 ml) orange juice

4 fl oz (110 ml) grapefruit juice

artificial sweetener to taste

4 standard egg whites

Dissolve the gelatine in 4 tablespoons hot water. Add to juice and stir well. Add sweetener to taste. Whisk egg whites until stiff peaks form. Fold into gelatine mixture. Divide evenly between 4 individual dessert bowls. Chill well before serving.

NB When this dessert is used, the egg yolk must be eaten at the same meal.

Makes 4 servings

Queen of Puddings

2½ fl oz (70 ml) skim milk

artificial sweetener to taste

1 slice white bread (1 oz, 30 g)

1 standard egg, separated

2 teaspoons low-calorie strawberry jam

Preheat oven to 350°F, Gas Mark 4, 180°C. Warm the milk gently in a small saucepan. Add sweetener to taste. Crumble bread into an ovenproof dish. Pour warm milk over the bread and leave for 10 minutes. Stir in the egg yolk. Bake for 15–20 minutes. Whisk the egg white until stiff with sweetener to taste. Turn oven heat up to 400°F, Gas Mark 6, 200°C. Spread jam over the bread and top with the whisked egg white. Bake for about 8 minutes or until golden.

Makes 1 serving

Pineapple Upside Down Cake

8 slices canned pineapple, no sugar added, with 8 tablespoons juice

4 standard eggs, separated

artificial sweetener to taste

2 slices white bread (2 oz, 60 g) made into crumbs

12 teaspoons self-raising flour

4 portions Weight Watchers Frozen Vanilla Dessert

Preheat oven to 425°F, Gas Mark 7, 220°C. Arrange pineapple rings in the base of a 7" cake tin. Mix the juice, egg yolks, sweetener, breadcrumbs and flour. Beat egg whites until stiff and fold into yolk mixture. Pour over pineapple and bake for 25 minutes or until risen and golden brown. Turn out onto serving dish, divide into 4 equal portions and serve each immediately with a portion of Weight Watchers Frozen Vanilla Dessert.

Makes 4 servings

Orange Delight

4 tablespoons undiluted low-calorie orange drink

½ tablespoon lemon juice

1 teaspoon unflavoured gelatine

10 oz (280 g) cottage cheese

3 fl oz (80 ml) buttermilk

1 medium orange, sliced

Pour orange drink and lemon juice into a small bowl and sprinkle gelatine on top. Stand the bowl in a pan of hot water and heat gently until gelatine is dissolved, stirring well. Transfer to blender, add cheese and buttermilk. Blend until smooth. Divide mixture between 2 dessert dishes and decorate with equal amounts of orange slices.

Makes 2 servings

Sauces for Desserts

Custard Sauce

3 teaspoons cornflour

10 fl oz (280 ml) skim milk

¼ teaspoon vanilla flavouring

¼ teaspoon yellow food colouring

artificial sweetener to taste

Mix the cornflour with 2 tablespoons skim milk. In a saucepan, combine remaining milk, vanilla flavouring, yellow food colouring and sweetener, add cornflour and gradually bring to the boil. Cook, stirring all the time, for 2 minutes. Serve hot or cold. Divide evenly.

Makes 2 servings

Chocolate Sauce

4 tablespoons margarine

2 oz (60 g) nonfat dry milk

artificial sweetener to taste

2 teaspoons chocolate Colour Flavouring

½ teaspoon vanilla flavouring

6 tablespoons warm water

2 teaspoons unsweetened cocoa powder

Beat margarine and dry milk together in a basin until well mixed. Gradually add warm water and rest of ingredients. Beat all together for 1 minute and serve with desserts, at mealtime only. Divide evenly.
(See p. 139 for serving suggestion).

Makes 4 servings

Breakfasts

Breakfasts

Gypsy Toast

1 standard egg

1 slice white bread (1 oz, 30 g)

3 oz (80 g) mixed mushrooms and tomatoes, cooked

salt and pepper to taste

Beat egg and pour onto a plate. Dip both sides of bread in the egg until it is completely absorbed. Dry-fry the bread in a non-stick pan. Garnish with mushrooms and tomatoes and season to taste.

Makes 1 serving

Muesli

½ oz (15 g) uncooked porridge oats

½ oz (15 g) cornflakes

2 medium prunes, soaked and chopped

½ medium red eating apple

2 fl oz (60 ml) natural unsweetened yogurt

2 teaspoons sesame seeds

5 fl oz (140 ml) skim milk

Mix first 6 ingredients together and serve with the skim milk.

Makes 1 serving

Fruit and Cereal Breakfast

4 oz (110 g) instant porridge oats

1 medium red apple, peeled

1 medium orange

4 oz (110 g) canned grapefruit sections, no sugar added

9 oz (260 g) chopped rhubarb

artificial sweetener to taste

1 pint (570 ml) skim milk

Place oats in large bowl, core and dice apple. Peel orange and dice, weigh grapefruit sections. Mix fruits with the oats, sprinkle with artificial sweetener. Mix again and divide evenly between 4 cereal bowls. Pour 5 fl oz (140 ml) milk over each and serve.

Makes 4 servings

Banana Wheat Breakfast

5 fl oz (140 ml) skim milk

½ medium banana

1 oz (30 g) wheat flakes

Pour skim milk into a blender and add to it ½ medium banana, sliced. Blend until liquefied, pour over the wheatflakes and serve.

Makes 1 serving

Peach and Cottage Cheese Salad

2 medium peaches

lemon juice

5 oz (140 g) cottage cheese

lettuce

3 oz (80 g) cucumber

2 tablespoons mayonnaise

Peel, halve and stone the peaches, brush the cut surfaces with lemon juice. Fill cavities with cottage cheese. Arrange a bed of crisp lettuce leaves on 2 serving plates. Grate the cucumber and arrange it on the lettuce. Sprinkle with more lemon juice. Place 2 stuffed peach halves on each plate. Spoon 1 tablespoon mayonnaise over each peach.

Makes 2 servings

Haddock and Tomatoes

3 oz (80 g) smoked haddock fillet

2 oz (60 g) tomatoes, grilled

1 hard roll

3 teaspoons margarine

Place haddock fillet in small non-stick frying pan, cover with water and slowly bring to boil. Cook for 1-2 minutes or until fish flakes easily with a fork. Lift fish out carefully with slotted spoon and serve with grilled tomatoes, hard roll and margarine.

Makes 1 serving

Pineapple Porridge

4 fl oz (110 ml) water

pinch salt

1 oz (30 g) porridge oats

4 oz (100 g) canned crushed pineapple, no sugar added

$\frac{1}{4}$ teaspoon cinnamon

artificial sweetener to taste

5 fl oz (140 ml) skim milk

Bring water to the boil in a small pan. Add salt and sprinkle in the porridge oats. Cook and stir over moderate heat for 1 minute. Remove from heat, cover and let stand for 30 seconds. Stir pineapple, cinnamon and sweetener into cooked cereal. Serve with skim milk.

Makes 1 serving

Omelette with Mushrooms and Peppers

$1\frac{1}{2}$ oz (45 g) green pepper

$1\frac{1}{2}$ oz (45 g) mushrooms

1 standard egg

salt and pepper to taste

1 slice bread (1 oz, 30 g) toasted

Dice green pepper, slice mushrooms and cook in salted water for 2-3 minutes, or until vegetables are tender but still crisp. Drain and keep hot. Beat egg. Heat a small non-stick frying pan, sprinkle base with a little salt, carefully pour in egg, tilt pan so egg covers base. Cook until bottom is set, turn over and brown other side. Slide onto warm plate, fill with peppers and mushrooms and serve at once, with slice of toast.

Makes 1 serving

Drinks

Drinks can be thirst quenching, cooling, warming or soothing, just as you wish. An informal drinks get-together with friends is also one of the nicest ways to entertain, and you'll be surprised at the variety of delicious recipes available when you are following the Weight Watchers Programme. You can base drinks on fruit and vegetable juices, on tea or coffee, even enjoy the flavour of chocolate all within the Weight Watchers Programme. In the summer, take some of your servings of fresh fruit in the form of drinks, and dress them up with good-looking glasses and sometimes a garnish of fruit slices or a sprig of herbs. The blender will help you to turn out smooth, professional looking sodas and shakes, so be prepared to make enough for all the family – you'll certainly have to once the children have tried a taste.

Drinks

Tea House Punch

$\frac{1}{4}$ teaspoon nutmeg

$\frac{1}{4}$ teaspoon allspice

$\frac{1}{4}$ teaspoon cinnamon

1 pint (570 ml) boiling water

3 tea bags

squeeze of lemon juice

$\frac{1}{4}$ teaspoon orange flavouring

1 pint (570 ml) cold water

artificial sweetener to taste

Combine nutmeg, allspice, cinnamon and hot water in saucepan. Bring to boil over medium heat. Boil for 1 minute and remove from heat. Add tea bags, steep for 5 minutes, strain, add lemon juice, orange flavouring, cold water and sweetener. Mix well. Serve chilled.

Makes 4 servings

Piquant Tomato Highball

1 pint (570 ml) tomato juice

2 sticks celery, roughly chopped

3-4 sprigs watercress

1 oz (30 g) cucumber, chopped

2-4 teaspoons Worcester sauce

artificial sweetener to taste

2-3 drops red food colouring

4 ice cubes

pepper and garlic salt to taste

4 sprigs watercress for garnish

4 sticks celery heart for garnish

Place half tomato juice in blender with rest of ingredients. Blend at high speed until reduced to a fine purée. Strain into jug, add rest of tomato juice and mix well. Divide evenly between 4 tall glasses and garnish each with watercress sprig and celery stick. Serve at once.

Makes 4 servings

Chocolate Milk Shake

10 fl oz (280 ml) skim milk

2 teaspoons unsweetened cocoa powder

2-3 drops vanilla flavouring

3 ice cubes

artificial sweetener to taste

Place all ingredients in blender and blend at high speed for 30 seconds. Pour into tall glass.

Makes 1 serving

Ginger Mint Cooler

8 fl oz (230 ml) water

artificial sweetener to taste

mint leaves

6 fl oz (170 ml) orange juice

4 fl oz (110 ml) lemon juice

8 fl oz (230 ml) low-calorie ginger ale

Combine water, sweetener and mint leaves. Bring to boil, strain and cool. Add to the other ingredients. Divide between 3 tall glasses and add crushed ice.

Makes 3 servings

Fruit Squash

½ grapefruit

1 medium orange

1 lemon

1½ pints (scant litre) water

2 tablespoons citric acid

artificial sweetener to taste

Peel fruit thinly. Place peel in blender together with the pulp and juice, but without any pips or white pith. Add 10 fl oz (280 ml) water and blend at full speed for 1 minute. Pour into a saucepan with 1 pint (570 ml) water and the citric acid. Bring to the boil and simmer for 5 minutes. Strain. When cold, add sweetener to taste and bottle.

Makes 4 servings

Caribbean Cocktail

8 fl oz (230 ml) low-calorie carbonated bitter lemon drink

12 fl oz (340 ml) grapefruit juice

few drops rum flavouring

artificial sweetener to taste

8 fl oz (230 ml) low-calorie ginger ale

juice of ½ lemon

1 medium orange, peeled and cut into dice

few sprigs mint

Place all ingredients, except mint, in blender. Blend, strain and divide between 4 glasses. Decorate with sprigs of mint.

Makes 4 servings

Bedtime Drink

1 oz (30 g) nonfat dry milk

¼ teaspoon salt, or to taste

½ teaspoon ground nutmeg, or to taste

Place all ingredients in a cup and mix to a paste with cold water. Add hot water to fill cup and stir.

Makes 1 serving

Fresh Peach Soda

5 fl oz (140 ml) soda water

3 tablespoons skim milk

1 portion Weight Watchers Frozen Vanilla Dessert

1 fresh medium peach, peeled, stoned and chopped

few drops maraschino or kirsch flavouring

artificial sweetener to taste

3-4 ice cubes

Place soda water, milk and Vanilla Dessert in blender. Blend for 1 minute, add the rest of the ingredients and blend for approximately 1 minute longer. Serve at once.

Makes 1 serving

Chocolate Delicious

1 teaspoon unsweetened cocoa powder

5 fl oz (140 ml) skim milk

1 portion Weight Watchers Frozen Vanilla Dessert

1 teaspoon chocolate Colour Flavouring

artificial sweetener to taste

Mix cocoa powder to a paste with 2-3 teaspoons milk. Place all ingredients in blender and blend for 1 minute. Serve in tall slim glass.

Makes 1 serving

Black Cherry Dream

10 large black cherries

5 fl oz (140 ml) skim milk

artificial sweetener to taste

3-4 ice cubes

Stone cherries and place in blender with all other ingredients. Blend until smooth. Serve at once.

Makes 1 serving

Left: Chocolate Delicious
Middle: Black Cherry Dream
Right: Fresh Peach Soda

Drinks

Orange Flip

2-3 ice cubes

8 fl oz (230 ml) low-calorie carbonated orange drink

1 oz (30 g) nonfat dry milk

Place 2-3 ice cubes in a tall glass. Mix orange and milk powder together thoroughly and pour over ice cubes.

Makes 1 serving

Quick and Easy Drink

½ medium banana

1 portion Weight Watchers Frozen Vanilla Dessert

10 fl oz (280 ml) skim milk

Place all ingredients in blender goblet and blend for 2 minutes or until light and frothy. Pour into tall glass and serve at once.

Makes 1 serving

Ginger-Lime Refresher

1 tablespoon low-calorie lime drink, undiluted

ice cubes

8 fl oz (230 ml) low-calorie ginger ale

Put lime drink and ice cubes into a tall glass, and top up with ginger ale.

Makes 1 serving

Cool Mint Lemon-Limeade

2 fl oz (60 ml) fresh lemon juice

2 fl oz (60 ml) low-calorie lime drink, undiluted

artificial sweetener to taste

few drops green food colouring

8 ice cubes

1½ pints (850 ml) soda water, chilled

4 sprigs mint

Mix together the lemon juice, lime drink, sweetener and food colouring. Place 2 ice cubes in each of 4 tall glasses, divide drink evenly between the glasses and top up with soda water. Decorate with sprigs of mint.

Makes 4 servings

Homemade Lemonade

1 lemon

5 fl oz (140 ml) cold water

boiling water as needed

artificial sweetener to taste

Peel the lemon thinly. Place peel in blender goblet and add the juice and flesh, but not the pips or white pith. Blend with cold water until all ingredients are finely chopped. Pour into a measuring jug and make up to 1 pint with boiling water. Leave overnight. Strain and add sweetener to taste.

Makes 2 servings

Pink Lady

8 fl oz (230 ml) skim milk

½ teaspoon rum flavouring

artificial sweetener to taste

3-4 ice cubes

Mix all ingredients thoroughly and serve in a tall glass.

Makes 1 serving

Pineapple Float

10 fl oz (280 ml) skim milk

8 oz (230 g) canned crushed pineapple, no sugar added

4 ice cubes

2 portions Weight Watchers Frozen Vanilla Dessert

Place all ingredients except Vanilla Dessert in blender and blend at high speed for 30 seconds. Divide evenly between 2 tall glasses, add one portion of Vanilla Dessert to each glass and serve immediately.

Makes 2 servings

Hints and Tips

Matchmates for fruit drinks: mint or cucumber for lemon drinks, spices like cloves and cinnamon to go with orange.

● Old fashioned borage will grow easily in your garden. Use the cucumber-flavoured leaves and the blue flower heads to decorate a jug of lemonade or fruit punch.

● If you are cutting up fruits such as apple or banana for drinks, toss the peeled fruits in lemon juice to prevent them from turning brown.

● Almost all soft fruits make delicious milk shakes, but the blender cannot dissolve the pips. Strain the drink through a fine sieve before serving.

● It's easy to add too much concentrated flavouring to a drink. Mix the drops of flavouring with a little of the milk or fruit juice, then add it gradually, tasting as you go.

● Fresh fruit drinks should be made just before serving, particularly if they are mixed with milk, or they may discolour and separate.

157